The Caddisfly Handbook

The Caddisfly Handbook
AN ORVIS GUIDE

DICK POBST
and
CARL RICHARDS

The Lyons Press

Printed in Canada
10 9 8 7 6 5 4 3 2 1

Design by V&M Graphics, Inc.

Library of Congress Cataloging-in-Publication Data

Pobst, Dick.
    The caddisfly handbook: an Orvis guide / Dick Pobst
and Carl Richards.
        p.   cm.
    Includes bibliographical references.
    ISBN 1-55821-542-5
    1. Fly fishing—United States.   2. Caddisflies—United
States.   I. Richards, Carl, 1933–   . II. Title.
SH463.P635   1999
799.1′24—dc21   98-8201
                                                        CIP

CONTENTS

Acknowledgments   vii

Introduction   1

     Finding the Really Important Hatches   1

     The Importance of Behavior   2

     Scientific Names or Common Names   3

1 The Caddis Rivers   5

     Tailwaters   5

     Trout Streams   6

     Spring Creeks   7

     No Two Rivers Are Alike   7

     The Muskegon   7

2 The Life Cycle of the Caddisfly   9

3 Identifying the Caddisflies   15

     First, Identify the Larvae or Cases   15

     Second, Identify the Adults   20

4 Major Caddisflies
West of the Mississippi   23

     Mother's Day Caddis—*Brachycentrus*   24

     Spotted Sedge—*Ceratopsyche/Hydropsyche*   26

     Little Sister Sedge—*Cheumatopsyche*   30

     Short-Horn Sedge—*Glossosoma*   32

     Weedy Water Sedge—*Micrasema/Amiocentrus*   34

     Speckled Peter—*Helicopsyche*   36

     Green Sedge—*Rhyacophila*   38

Little Brown Sedge—*Lepidostoma* 40
Gray-Winged Long-Horn Sedge—*Oecetis* 42
Black Dancer—*Mystacides* 44
Great Gray-Spotted Sedge—*Arctopsyche* 46
Great Silver-Striped Sedge—*Hesperophylax* 48
Giant Orange Sedge—*Dicosmoecus* 50
Trout Lake Caddis 52

5 Major Hatches East of the Mississippi **57**
Black Caddis—*Brachycentrus* 58
Cinnamon Caddis—*Ceratopsyche* 60
Little Olive Caddis—*Cheumatopsyche* 64
Dark Blue Sedge—*Psilotreta* 68
Green Sedge—*Rhyacophila* 70
Short-Horn Sedge—*Glossosoma* 72
Tiny Black Caddis—*Micrasema* 74
Zebra Caddis—*Macrostemum* 76
Tan-Winged Long-Horn Sedge—*Oecetis* 78
Dark Long-Horn Sedge—*Ceraclea* 80
White Miller—*Nectopsyche* 82
Dot-Winged Sedge—*Frenesia* 84
Great Brown Autumn Sedge—*Pycnopsyche* 86

6 Tying Caddis Imitations **88**

7 Master List of Caddis Patterns **94**

8 Occasionally Important Caddisflies **100**

Fisherman's Simplified Keys **102**

Bibliography **131**

Photographic Credits **133**

Personal Hatch Record **134**

Index **145**

ACKNOWLEDGMENTS

We would like to thank the many people who helped us in this venture:

Dr. Brian Armitage of the Ohio Biological Survey, for identifying many caddisfly specimens.

Dr. Richard Merritt of Michigan State University, coeditor of *Aquatic Insects of North America.*

Jeff Cooper of the Michigan Water Resources Commission, for help in identifying specimens.

Larry Solomon and Eric Leiser, authors of *Caddis and the Angler.*

Gary LaFontaine, author of *Caddisflies.*

John Juracek and Craig Mathews, authors of *Fishing the Yellowstone Hatches*, for advice and slides.

John Shewey, author of *Mastering the Spring Creeks.*

Jim Schollmeyer, author of *Hatches of the Deschutes*, for slides of the insects.

Bob Braendle, coauthor of *Caddis Super Hatches.*

Ted Fauceglia, author and photographer, for slides of the insects.

Hank Leonhard, for the use of his slides.

Dave Hughes, author and photographer, for advice and slides.

Rick Hafele, author, angler, and entomologist, for his advice and identifications.

Jason Kuipers and Jay Allen, for tying prototype flies.

Robert McKeon, artist and illustrator, who did the black-and-white drawings.

Lindsey Wells, artist, who did the black-and-white drawings for the Fisherman's Keys.

Our wives, Alecia Richards and Nancy Pobst, for their critiques and suggestions.

Nick Lyons, of the Lyons Press, and Frank Amato, of Frank Amato Publications.

The host of anglers and friends who helped with questions along the way.

INTRODUCTION

My coauthor, Carl Richards, started fishing Michigan's Muskegon River in 1959, and he introduced me to it in the mid-1970s. This river had terrific caddisfly hatches but no one could consistently catch fish, even when they were feeding on the caddis all around us.

When we did catch fish we took some fat, strong, well-conditioned trout, for the river is rich in caddis. Twelve-inch fish shaped like footballs would put up a great fight, and the larger 19-inch cruisers could keep anyone's adrenaline going all evening. There were plenty of fish, and plenty of bugs, but we could not sort out which flies the fish were taking, and we were frequently skunked.

Caddis and the Angler, by Larry Solomon and Eric Leiser, and *Caddisflies*, by Gary LaFontaine, provided considerable information—more information than we could actually process. *Caddisflies* listed some 193 species, a small portion of the existing species. We would certainly never learn to fish all these. For a long time it seemed that the more we learned, the more difficult the puzzle became.

We turned to academia to learn more about caddisflies. We found shelf after shelf of scholarly papers on the insects, but most of the papers provided little information about color, size, or behavior of these flies. And they listed over 1,000 species, so the problem of sorting out the hatches got worse.

Finding the Really Important Hatches

A few years ago, we began to doubt there were many important hatches—that is, important enough for the fish to feed steadily and regularly on them. So we collected samples from the Muskegon River and sent them to Richard Merritt of the Michigan State University Entomology Department. This time we said: "We do not want an analysis of every insect—only those that occur in great numbers."

After a summer of submitting specimens, we got our answer: There are only two species of any real importance during the summer. Carl then began a more exhaustive study and confirmed that there are two major hatches on the Muskegon, plus a few of secondary importance.

After several seasons of continuing investigation, we finally concluded that about four genera of caddis constitute up to three-quarters of the fishable hatches in the United States. There are a dozen of secondary importance, and probably no more than 50 species in the entire country of significance. Contrast that with the aforementioned 1,000 species, or even the 193!

The Importance of Behavior

Once we were able to narrow the list, we turned our attention to determining how to figure out which stage of the insect life cycle we were fishing to. This is far more difficult with caddis than with mayflies, and far more important. Mayflies undergo a physical change from dun to spinner, so one glance will tell you if you are fishing to an emergence or a spinner fall, but caddisflies do not change between emergence and egg laying. If you see a caddisfly off the water you won't know if it has just emerged from the pupa or if it's a female returning from the bottom after egg laying, because they look alike. Furthermore, most mayflies lay their eggs on the surface, while most caddisflies oviposit (lay eggs) underwater. We had to learn the habits of the various genera because their behavior can vary considerably, even though the forms may look alike. It is vital to know these differences to fish each successfully.

We learned that most caddisfly pupae swim to the surface using their middle legs in breaststroke fashion, but some crawl out of the water to hatch. Once reaching the surface, they may drift for considerable distances attached to the underside of the surface film, or they may break the surface film immediately and begin struggling out of their pupal shucks. The insects will drift from 5 to 30 feet during the struggle. A good pupal imitation is effective when the natural pupae are drifting under the surface, but an emerger is a killer when trout are feeding on emergers. Once the wings are out, most caddisflies flap them once or twice, then fly away. The adult pattern is thus less effective than a pupa or emerger because the natural adult is not easily available to the fish. However, the adult pattern is effective when the fish are feeding on adult females swimming back to the surface after egg laying.

Scientific Names or Common Names

Often the common names of the caddis are not widely used. Some are cumbersome, such as *dinky purple-breasted sedge*. Names like *sedge* and *grannom* have no specific meaning. On the other hand, Latin names are hard to remember, and they intimidate people. We have decided to include both; use the one you find more helpful. As for pronunciation of Latin names, just try your closest approximation of Italian or Spanish, as if reading a menu. Latin teachers, scientists, and priests all use different pronunciations. No one alive has ever heard a native speak Latin, so the next person does not know any more about it than you do. Besides, the names are not purely Latin; they're a mixture of Latin, Greek, and a whole lot of other things.

We have taken some liberties, however, with the common names. We have tended to use *tiny black caddis* for many #20 black caddis forms, since that is the way we first notice them, rather than *short-horn* or *weedy water sedge* names. We have used *long-horn* to distinguish those caddisflies with long antennae, since those antennae are their most obvious characteristic. And we have tended to prefer *cinnamon caddis* to *spotted sedge*, because it seems more descriptive. In most cases we have given more than one name.

Chapter 1

THE CADDIS RIVERS

Much of our caddis research has focused on whether there is a pattern to where and when caddisflies reach major hatch proportions. We found that some rivers, such as the Muskegon in Michigan, are mainly caddis rivers. Much of the summer you must know the caddisflies to fish these rivers. Other rivers, however, such as the Clinch in Tennessee, are mainly mayfly rivers, with only a few caddis species. What is the difference? There is no single answer to this question that covers all streams.

Tailwaters

Caddisflies appear in significant quantities most often on tailwaters and large trout streams. This is important because most of the largest trout streams in the country are tailwaters. Michigan's Muskegon, Manistee, and Au Sable, below their dams, meet all the requirements, and they do have huge hatches of caddisflies. So do the Madison and Missouri in the West, as well as the great tailwaters of the Tennessee Valley Authority. We believe trout eat more caddisflies than mayflies in these tailwaters, but studies are rare and difficult to interpret.

Some rivers are fed by natural lakes and have great hatches of caddis; these should be classified with the tailwaters. The Yellowstone is a prime example. So one category of caddis rivers is warm-water tailwaters—rivers fed by top-spill dams or natural lakes.

When water is released from the base of the dam and where a deep reservoir of cold water exists, other tailwaters may have colder water temperatures, such as the Bighorn in Montana, and the South Holston and Clinch in Tennessee. These rivers produce more mayflies and fewer caddisflies than do warmer rivers. Temperature is undoubtedly a factor in determining which insects thrive in which places.

We believe the major factor, though, is that lakes—natural or artificial—produce large quantities of plankton near the surface; this plankton is fed into rivers by top-spill dams and natural lakes, but not so much from bottom-release dams. The most important caddisflies feed largely on plankton, and therefore thrive in the top-fed rivers. These are the Hydropsychidae, about which more will be said later.

Trout Streams

There is one major group of flies, however, that does not rely solely on plankton. This is the black caddis, or Mother's Day caddis *(Brachycentrus)*. They thrive in cold water, and usually hatch during the cold early trout season. They are most common in undammed trout streams but will hatch in some tailwaters during spring periods of cold water.

Trout streams do not regularly produce the huge caddis hatches that occur in tailwaters, but there are significant hatches—which are frequently ignored by anglers because the mayfly hatches are so much easier to detect and analyze. As you become more familiar with the caddis populations of your trout streams, you will find many more opportunities to fish them.

Small, woodsy brook trout streams produce few mayflies but lots of caddis. The brook trout in these streams consume more caddis than mayflies.

Spring Creeks

The classic spring creeks, such as those of the Yellowstone Valley, produce huge quantities of mayflies and far fewer caddis. Their colder water and decreased amount of plankton are probably factors.

No Two Rivers Are Alike

It is really necessary to analyze each river separately, because most rivers do not fit neatly into a simple category. For example, the Henry's Fork is fed by both springs and lakes, and has variations in gradient and structure that make it difficult to categorize. It also hosts just about every kind of fly known to anglers. Don't try to oversimplify.

The Muskegon

A few years ago Michigan became the first state in which it was necessary to relicense major hydroelectric dams. This process fell under the jurisdiction of the Federal Energy Regulatory Commission, and would result in new licenses valid for 50 years. There have been huge conflicts between power companies and fisheries managers over the operation of the dams. This is a big story in itself.

Since we fish the Muskegon regularly, we were concerned about what would happen. We spoke to Gary Whelan of the Michigan Department of Natural Resources, and asked him why they did not just leave the Muskegon alone.

Gary told us that if the dam operation was changed to natural-flow levels—run-of-the-river—rather than running in peaks to generate electricity, we would see huge increases in the production of aquatic insects. Constant fluctuations in water levels scour food from the water, so that only a few forms of aquatic insects can survive.

He said that equally important is the fact that constantly changing water levels provide no shallow-water nurseries for small trout, so they are eaten every time they are forced into the deep holes with the bigger fish.

The Muskegon's flow levels *were* changed, and both of Gary's predictions proved true. We now have more caddis, plus a burgeoning number of mayfly hatches—six new species at last count—and some stoneflies where they were rare before.

The Colorado River at Lee's Ferry has been through a similar process. It had few hatches when we fished it a few years ago, when water levels varied by several feet every day. We recently learned that the dam at Flaming Gorge Reservoir on the Green River no longer alters its levels so drastically, and understand that the insect hatches have improved considerably.

It seems that great improvements could be made in many tailwater fisheries if proper natural-flow regulations were implemented.

Chapter 2

THE LIFE CYCLE OF THE CADDISFLY

The purpose of this book is to make the caddisflies understandable, and therefore fishable. Like love and marriage, you can't have one without the other. To fish caddis hatches, you need to understand the caddis life cycle.

Female caddisflies lay eggs on the surface; by hitting the surface and diving to the bottom; or by crawling to the river's edge or onto pilings then diving to the bottom. It is most important for the fisherman to know which genera use which methods of laying eggs.

The behavior of the larvae is complicated enough to be the subject of an entire book, but a few points are of major importance to the angler.

Caddis larva

The most numerous flies are the Hydropsychidae, which build nets to trap food. Most of the other major genera build cases. The exceptions are the Rhyacophilidae and some relatively minor families. Caddisflies have the ability to spin silklike fibers from their mouths. They use these fibers to build cases like cocoons, to build webs, or to rappel from one spot to another.

Caddis case

There are times when trout grub for larvae on the bottom. But the flies are only available in quantity during what scientists call behavioral drift, and during the cycle of emergence–egg laying–dying. Richard Merritt and Ken Cummins, noted entomologists, stated in a letter: "Feeding activity of trout occurs in connection with two major events: 1) the emergence behavior of aquatic insects, including the preemergence drift of nymphs and emerging adults, and egg-laying adults; and 2) during the major (dawn and dusk) drift periods."

Most behavioral drift occurs just before dawn and just after dusk. Usually the drifting larvae are without cases. A drifting larva floats with its head down, so we suggest a beadhead fly, fished dead drift with a strike indicator, during the drift period.

All caddisflies turn into pupae to hatch. They do this either by sealing themselves in their existing cases, or by building a pupal case if they have no other. If you find caddis in sealed cases, they are going to emerge soon.

Caddis deposits eggs on water. Caddis dives to lay eggs then ascends. Spent caddis floats on surface.

Illustration by Robert McKeon

Caddis pupa swimming to the surface and emerging as an adult

Illustration by Robert McKeon

It is when the insects leave the pupal case and begin to emerge that the feeding cycle most exciting to anglers begins. Each stage of the emergence cycle causes the flies to be available in quantity and triggers major feeding activity by fish.

Caddis pupa

Some pupae drift along the bottom at first. These can be imitated by a beadhead pupa fished dead drift with a strike indicator.

All pupae eventually swim upward, using their legs to breaststroke their way to the surface. This is the point at which a pupa tied with a few strands of sparse soft hackle works well; fish it upward and with movement to make the legs swim.

When the pupae arrive at the surface they frequently appear to drift just beneath the surface film, so close they are almost touching. In many cases their backs are actually attached to the surface film. This is the first stage at which the flies are collected into one spot in quantity and (from the fish's perspective) silhouetted against the sky. At this point they are extremely vulnerable to fish. Their legs, wings, cases, and antennae are visible under their bodies. The pupae appear practically inert, in what we call the tuck position.

In some cases they drift for several feet. In others they quickly work through the surface film and struggle to escape the pupal shuck. At such times, we fish a pupa tied as an emerger with a shuck attached.

Pupal shuck

In any event, as soon as the flies are free of their shucks, they quickly fly away. They are not readily available to fish as emerged adults.

Mating caddis

After the flies reach the streamside bushes they mate without further change, and the females return to the river to lay their eggs. A female may lay eggs two, three, or more times during her life. An adult caddis pattern fished under the surface film or on the surface, depending on the egg-laying method in question, will work at this stage.

Spentwing caddis

Finally, after laying eggs for the last time, the females fall spent on the surface. We have experienced major feeding activity on spentwing caddis after dark or at dawn during the Hydropsychidae season.

The fish feed in calm, flat water and are extremely selective. There have been times when the only way we could hook a fish was to set the hook in anticipation of the strike. Here is how it works: When a fish is feeding selectively and rising in the same spot, make a mental note of the spot, no matter that the ring of the rise drifts downstream. Then cast a foot upstream of the spot. At the instant the fly drifts within an inch of the spot, raise the rod. With luck, the fish will take the fly just as you tighten the line. Otherwise, the fish would spit out your fly before you could set the hook. We have never figured out why they will reject so quickly sometimes and take so solidly at others.

Now you need to discover which insect you are fishing, so that you can make your fly act like the natural. When you are uncertain whether the fish are taking the pupa, the emerger, or the adult that has just laid eggs, fish an adult caddis with a floating pupa dropper. If the fish fail to take either, tug the line to sink the dry fly and it will imitate the emerging egg layer.

Chapter 3

IDENTIFYING THE CADDISFLIES

To understand caddisflies, concentrate on two facts.

First, two groups of flies make up the vast majority of significant caddis hatches: the black caddis of the springtime *(Brachycentrus)* and the cinnamon caddis and its cousin, the little olive caddis, of the summertime (Hydropsychidae).

Second, the significant hatches of North America can be boiled down to about 20 genera, all of which are easily identifiable from their cases, or from their larvae if they have no cases. Probably no more than a half dozen are significant on your stream.

Once you recognize those 20 larval forms, you can tell what caddis hatches will occur in your waters.

First, Identify the Larvae or Cases

Stick to those specimens that are numerous. (A blank hatch chart, which can be copied, is printed on page 134, and you can list any numerous specimens you find.)

Start by picking up rocks and logs to find the cased larvae, which are mainly attached thereto.

Then seine gravel—the same way you would for mayfly nymphs, but with a few refinements. Seining will collect the caddis that do not build cases.

Cinnamon Caddis and Little Olive Caddis
Family Hydropsychidae

Our estimate is that these flies may equal 40 to 50 percent or more of the fishable caddis. Concentrate on these first groups and your time will be well spent. This is the most complicated set of flies, scientifically speaking, but it boils down to two important ones:

1. The cinnamon caddis—#16 hook—made up of *Hydropsyche* and *Ceratopsyche* genera. *(Ceratopsyche were recently reclassified from Hydropsyche.)*

2. The little olive caddis—#18 hook—genus *Cheumatopsyche*.

All these flies are easily identified if you remember that the larva has three dark plates on the first three body segments behind its head (see illustration).

This group is composed of closely related members of the family Hydropsychidae. They are the most important of all caddisflies and dominate in the summer months, especially on tailwaters and large rivers, although they are also found on smaller streams. The larvae can be easily captured by seining riffles.

The pupae emerge in midstream. Females lay their eggs either by swimming underwater (more than half) or by sprawling and bouncing on the surface. The adults can be identified by the straight trailing edge of their forewings. It is the predominance, similar behavior, and daytime emergence of these flies that make them so important. Two hook sizes and two colors imitate them all.

These flies build nets among the gravel to trap food, which consists of plankton. Plankton is mostly produced in lakes, above dams, and in warm-water pools in big rivers. This central fact accounts for Hydropsychidae being the most numerous flies in tailwaters and rivers fed by lakes.

Additionally, they are among the few flies that can survive in rivers where water levels are drastically raised and lowered, an action that wipes out the habitat of many other aquatic insects.

Little Black Caddis
Genus *Brachycentrus*

In all parts of North America, early black caddis hatch from chimney tube cases, as pictured. They are typically imitated with #16 hooks.

In both East and West the black caddis is the first major caddis hatch of the season. This is the Mother's Day caddis of the Rocky Mountains and the black caddis of the East, and it creates major fishable hatches. *Brachycentrus* usually lay their eggs on the surface, like mayflies. They hatch most prevalently on undammed trout streams and bottom-release tailwaters because they need clear, cold water to survive. In each section of the country the initial hatch is followed by one or more relatives that live in the same sort of cases and same type of water. We estimate that these flies constitute around 20 percent of the fishable caddis.

Green Sedge
Genus *Rhyacophila*

This caddis is generally more important as a larva than as a dry fly. The green worms are often large and are an important part of the trout's (especially the steelhead's) diet. This caddis is so widespread that it cannot be ignored. It is the only major free-living caddisfly. It is easy to collect and identify. It can be distinguished from the *Hydropsyche* by the one light amber plate on the body segment behind its head, as compared to three dark ones. It usually does not emerge in a concentrated fashion, but egg-laying flights are sometimes massive and important. The females crawl underwater to oviposit. Emerging flies and escaping egg layers often skitter to shore after reaching the surface.

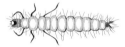

Most of the other major caddisflies are readily identified by the cases in which they spend most of their lives. When you visit a new river, you can determine which caddis hatches will be occurring by finding the cases or larvae. Following are illustrations you can use for that purpose. These can further be lumped into three categories:

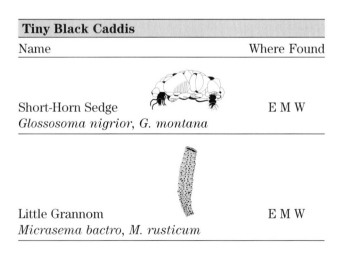

Tiny Black Caddis	
Name	Where Found
Short-Horn Sedge *Glossosoma nigrior, G. montana*	E M W
Little Grannom *Micrasema bactro, M. rusticum*	E M W

Name		Where Found

Speckled Peter   E M W
Helicopsyche borealis

Long-Horn Sedges

Long-Horn Sedge   E M W
Oecetis avara, O. disjuncta

Black Dancer   W
Mystacides alafimbriata,
M. sepulchralis

White Miller
Nectopsyche albida   E M

Dark Long-Horn Sedge   E
Ceraclea transversa

Others

Dark Blue Sedge   E
Psilotreta labida

Grannom   E M W
Brachycentrus americanus

Name		Where Found
Little Brown Sedge *Lepidostoma pluviale*	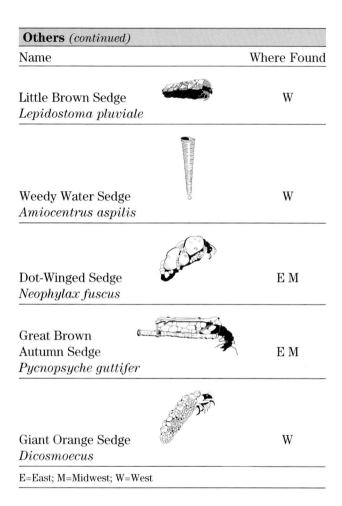	W
Weedy Water Sedge *Amiocentrus aspilis*		W
Dot-Winged Sedge *Neophylax fuscus*		E M
Great Brown Autumn Sedge *Pycnopsyche guttifer*		E M
Giant Orange Sedge *Dicosmoecus*		W

E=East; M=Midwest; W=West

Second, Identify the Adults

This will be easier if you have already identified the larvae or cases. For example, if you find a tiny black caddisfly and you already know *Glossosoma* cases are present in large numbers, you can deduce that this is what it is. Always catch the fly—never try to identify it in the air. To do so:

1. Use a fine-mesh net to strain the surface for emergers or egg layers. This may be a slow process; they are often widespread. What you catch, however, is probably what the fish are eating right now.

2. Use a long-handled net to sweep the grass and bushes along the stream. If a big hatch has occurred lately, you will easily capture many individuals.

3. Use a light trap at night to collect adults. Or make one, using a pan of alcohol under a light. Or just look in spiderwebs on buildings with lights on along rivers at night.

4. Carry a specimen bottle with acetone in it. The acetone will kill your specimen so it cannot escape while preserving its color.

Now use the cases, larvae, or adult specimens to find the correct fly in the following pages, which are organized by importance first in the West, then in the East.

For example, let's say you've found a bunch of cases in the river that look like this:

Page through the hatch chapters to find this case. When you do, you'll also find information about a hatch that will occur in your river this season (see page 36).

If you have a specimen of the adult, such as this one:

Helicopsyche borealis

You know that the hatch you predicted is happening now.

Chapter 4

MAJOR CADDISFLIES
WEST OF THE MISSISSIPPI

The western states have many miles of major rivers
that are suitable for trout. Many of these rivers are
dammed. Therefore, caddisflies are probably more
important here than they are in the eastern part of
the country.

Most of our hatch dates come from rivers in the
Yellowstone region, including the Yellowstone, the
Henry's Fork, and the Missouri. Hatches in higher ele-
vations will be later than on the Yellowstone. Hatches
at lower elevations will be earlier—in the Pacific
Northwest, for example.

Also note that some hatches in the mountain states
will be unfishable; the high water of snowmelt will take
these rivers out of the running.

Nevertheless, a huge portion of the great trout fishing in the world is to be had in the American West.

Western caddisflies are presented here approximately in their order of hatching. It also happens that
the first flies listed are the most important. These are
color-coded red. The next most important are coded
blue, and the rest yellow.

Mother's Day Caddis
(Black Caddis)

Brachycentrus occidentalis

Brachycentrus americanus

MOTHER'S DAY CADDIS
(BLACK CADDIS)
Family: Brachycentridae

Brachycentrus occidentalis—Peak: April–mid-May.

B. americanus—Peak: Late July–August.

These flies emerge in April and May at mid-day, from cold-water trout streams and cold tailwaters. Their characteristics are:

HOOK #16 (males one size smaller).

OVERALL LENGTH 8–13 millimeters.

BODY Dark gray with green or tan lateral line.

WINGS Gray with black veins.

LEGS Gray.

ANTENNAE Dark gray with lighter rings.

NOTE: *B. americanus* has a brownish cast and is larger (at 12–15 millimeters) than *B. occidentalis*. Its hatch peaks in late July, early August.

Brachycentrus case: The case of the little black caddis is known as a chimney case. It has a square cross section and is tapered. The cases can be found clinging to stones and wood; they are numerous before the hatch.

Mother's Day Caddis (Black Caddis)

Range: W, NW.

Habitat: Rocks or wood in cold trout streams.

Emergence: Midstream, midday.

Egg laying: Dips eggs on the surface in the afternoon.

The pupa, shown in the tuck position, often drifts many feet attached to the surface film before emerging.

ADULT IMITATION

WINGS Dark gray Fly Film.

BODY Dark gray dubbing.

HACKLE Gray.

ANTENNAE Dark gray hackle stem, stripped.

Brachycentrus Pupa

This is the year's first heavy emergence of caddisflies in the West, and trout feed heavily on it. The hatch usually occurs on undammed trout streams and bottom-release tailwaters. The flies begin emerging around midday, just before runoff begins. Egg laying is in the afternoon and can coincide with the emergence. Peak emergence occurs from the last half of April to mid-June, depending on the river. The adults drift up to 30 feet struggling from their pupal shucks. Once out, they may drift on the surface or fly away quickly. They oviposit much like mayflies, dipping their bodies onto the surface, although some individuals may crawl or dive underwater.

Adult imitation

Spotted Sedge
(Cinnamon Caddis)

Ceratopsyche cockerelli

Adult *Hydropsyche*

**SPOTTED SEDGE
(CINNAMON CADDIS)**
Family: Hydropsychidae

Ceratopsyche cockerelli, Hydropsyche occidentalis, H. oslari, H. placoda, et al.

Peak: All season; mostly afternoon and evening, but sometimes in the morning.

We prefer the name *cinnamon caddis* as more descriptive, since spots are not always evident.

These flies emerge from May to September, mainly during the evening in summer, but some earlier in the day. They are most important in tailwaters, but many are found in trout streams. Their characteristics are:

HOOK #16 (males one size smaller).

OVERALL LENGTH 9–13 millimeters.

BODY Cinnamon brown.

WINGS Brownish gray with a speckling of small tan spots.

LEGS Brown.

ANTENNAE Tan with dark rings.

Spotted Sedge
(Cinnamon Caddis)

Hydropsyche/Ceratopsyche larva: This larva is characterized by three dark plates on the body segments behind its head, as are its relatives in the family Hydropsychidae.

It builds a net like a spiderweb among the gravel to trap food. It does not build a case until it is ready to pupate, about two weeks before emergence.

Range: W, NW.

Habitat: Gravel riffles; most prolific on tailwaters.

Food: Builds a net to strain plankton from lakes.

Emergence: Midstream, mostly afternoon and evening.

Egg laying: Crawls or dives to the bottom, or sprawls on the surface.

Adult *Hydropsyche*

Spotted Sedge
(Cinnamon Caddis)

Adult imitation

The pupa, shown in the tuck position, often drifts many feet under the surface film before emerging.

ADULT IMITATION

WINGS Mottled tan and gray-brown grouse or quail body feathers.

BODY Cinnamon dubbing.

HACKLE Brown.

ANTENNAE Dark brown hackle stem, stripped.

This is by far the most important family for trout fishermen. Only in the early spring when little black caddis and tiny black caddis are on the water do any other caddisflies even come close in importance to this fly and its cousin, the little olive caddis.

They hatch in large numbers, usually in the evening but also in the morning, seemingly when the nights are very warm. Egg laying is done in the morning and evening, with some during the daytime.

These caddisflies may drift as pupae for a long time before their emergence. They also take a long time to struggle from their pupal shucks. These two factors allow you to hook a lot of fish long before the hatch begins on a pupal imitation fished dead drift on the bottom, as a floating pupa just under the surface film, or as an emerger. The pupae emerge in midstream.

The females crawl or dive underwater or sprawl on the surface to lay eggs. A surface-fished dry fly is often effective

Spotted Sedge
(Cinnamon Caddis)

during egg laying, or it can be pulled under the surface to imitate the returning egg-laying female.

Many spent caddis collect on the water after dark, and the fish will feed selectively on quad-wing patterns during that time.

Triple dropper rig

To find out which stage of the insect the fish are taking, tie on a floating fly; then tie a dropper from it and attach an emerger; then add a pupal imitation that will float just under the surface. Fish these dead drift. If the fish take one consistently, you know which fly to use.

If the fish rise all around your flies but do not take, pull the dry fly underwater. It may then be taken for an egg-laying female returning to the surface.

At the end of egg laying, fish will often take a spent imitation. A quad-wing fly or delta-wing fly will then work.

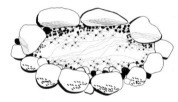

Temporary pupal case

NOTE: Those caddisflies that do not live in cases as larvae—such as this one—build cases briefly for a couple of weeks to change into pupae. You can easily tell one of these pupal cases from the normal larval case because it is open on one side, exposing the silk-encased pupa. When you take a knife and remove it from a rock, the entire pupa is exposed as if in a window (see illustration). *Rhyacophila* builds a similar case.

Little Sister Sedge
(Little Olive Caddis)

Cheumatopsyche lasia

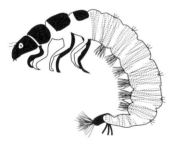

Cheumatopsyche larva: This larva is characterized by three dark plates on the body segments behind its head, as are its relatives in the family Hydropsychidae. It builds a net like a spiderweb among the gravel to trap food. It does not build a case until it is ready to pupate, about two weeks before emergence.

LITTLE SISTER SEDGE (LITTLE OLIVE CADDIS)
Family: Hydropsychidae

Cheumatopsyche pettiti, C. lasia, C. campyla—Peak: All season; mainly afternoon and evening, but morning in fall.

These flies emerge from May to September, mainly during the evening in summer, but some earlier in the day. They are most important in tailwaters, but some are found in trout streams. Their characteristics are:

HOOK #18 (males one size smaller).

OVERALL LENGTH 7.5 millimeters.

BODY Olive.

WINGS Brownish gray with a speckling of small tan areas.

LEGS Brown.

ANTENNAE Tan with dark rings.

Range: W, NW.

Habitat: Gravel riffles; most prolific in tailwaters.

Food: Plankton from warm tailwaters.

Emergence: Midstream.

Egg laying: Crawls or dives to the bottom, or sprawls on the surface.

The pupa often drifts many feet attached to the surface film before emerging.

Little Sister Sedge
(Little Olive Caddis)

ADULT IMITATION

WINGS Mottled tan and gray-brown grouse or quail body feathers.

BODY Olive.

HACKLE Brown.

ANTENNAE Dark brown hackle stem, stripped.

This is the second most important genus for trout fishermen, a close second to *Hydropsyche/Ceratopsyche,* to which it is closely related. Since these genera belong to the same family their habits, style of emergence, and egg laying are very similar, if not identical. They hatch and lay eggs at the same time of day, interspersed with the spotted sedge hatch.

Adult imitation in summer colors

These insects are similar in shape to spotted sedges and have the same unique wing shape. They are a little smaller than *Hydropsyche/Ceratopsyche,* and can easily be distinguished from them by their smaller size and olive body color. The few *Hydropsyche/Ceratopsyche* that have olive bodies at emergence (which quickly turn cinnamon or brown) are larger. These caddisflies become much lighter as the season progresses—as do many other species, but the little sister seems to exhibit this trait in the extreme. The wings, which are dark in the early season, become much lighter in the fall and appear white in flight. They emerge in the morning and evening, but can come at midday on cool, overcast days. Ovipositing is usually at dusk in the West.

Adult imitation in fall colors

The females dive underwater or sprawl on the surface to lay eggs. A surface-fished dry fly is often effective during egg laying, or it can be pulled under the surface to imitate the returning egg-laying female.

Many spent caddis collect on the water after dark, and the fish will feed selectively on quad-wing patterns at that time.

Temporary pupal case

31

Tiny Black Caddis
(Short-Horn Sedge)

Adult *Glossosoma Montana*

Glossosoma case

TINY BLACK CADDIS
(SHORT-HORN SEDGE)
Family: Glossosomatidae

Glossosoma montana—Peak: Spring and fall.

These flies emerge sporadically from spring to fall in trout streams, occasionally in large numbers, usually in the morning.

HOOK #20 (males one size smaller).

OVERALL LENGTH 6–7.5 millimeters.

BODY Black.

WINGS Black with a few light tan spots midwing and a few at the wing tips.

LEGS Dark gray.

ANTENNAE Black with light tan rings.

Glossosoma case: This is known as a domed saddle case. The larva takes the case with it as it moves along the surface of rocks.

Range: W, NW.

Habitat: Cold streams.

Emergence: Riffles, midstream.

Egg laying: Late afternoon, evening; dives in riffles.

Tiny Black Caddis
(Short-Horn Sedge)

ADULT IMITATION

WINGS Black hen hackle.

BODY Black dubbing.

HACKLE Gray.

ANTENNAE Black hackle stems, stripped.

Adult imitation

This is an important species because its members emerge all season long, usually a few at a time but occasionally in good numbers. They can cause heavy feeding when the emergence is large, and some rises when the hatch is light. Since these are small, dark forms, they are hard to see, but fish will feed on them. (You may notice that the trout are rising, but see nothing on the water.) The most important time for this hatch is during spring mornings, because not much else is emerging at this time.

The pupae emerge in midstream, and pupal and emerger imitations are effective. In the spring some pupae emerge in midstream and crawl on the surface of the water to shore. A hackled pupal imitation skittered on the surface is very effective at these times. Females submerge to oviposit.

Tiny Black Caddis
(Weedy Water Sedge, Little Grannom)

TINY BLACK CADDIS (WEEDY WATER SEDGE, LITTLE GRANNOM)
Family: Brachycentridae

Micrasema bactro—Peak (Yellowstone): late July–early August.

Amiocentrus aspilis—Peak (Bighorn): Spring and fall.

These caddis hatch from cold-water trout streams during June evenings. The Bighorn has emergences in May and September.

HOOK #20 (males one size smaller).

Micrasema bactro

OVERALL LENGTH 7–9 millimeters.

BODY Dark gray with green lateral line.

WINGS Black.

LEGS Dark gray.

ANTENNAE Dark gray with lighter rings.

Range: W, NW.

Habitat: Cold streams.

Emergence: Midstream.

Egg laying: Crawls or dives; lays green egg balls.

Amiocentrus aspilis

Tiny Black Caddis
(Weedy Water Sedge, Little Grannom)

Adult Imitation

WINGS Black hen hackle.

BODY Black dubbing.

HACKLE Gray.

ANTENNAE Black hackle stems, stripped.

These are important species because they emerge all season long, in good numbers. They cause heavy feeding when the emergence is large. Since these are small, dark forms, they are hard to see. (You may notice that the trout are rising, but see nothing on the water.)

Adult imitation

Another reason for the importance of these species is that the peak emergences in the West are concentrated and the caddis hatch in huge numbers, like the Mother's Day caddis, to which they are closely related. *M. bactro* emerges and oviposits during warm summer evenings on the Yellowstone River in the park. *A. aspilis* is the important species on the Bighorn and has two emergence periods, one in May, the other in September. This hatch is a daytime affair and produces some heavy, but selective, feeding.

Micrasema case

The pupae emerge in midstream and the adults fly off the water quickly, so a pupa or an emerger is the imitation of choice. Females crawl underwater or dip their bodies on the surface to lay eggs. The females that crawl underwater to oviposit swim back to the surface, where they float awash in the film. Adult imitations are best fished wet. Spentwing imitations should be used after egg laying.

Amiocentrus case

35

Tiny Black Caddis
(Speckled Peter)

Adult *Helicopsyche*

Helicopsyche case

TINY BLACK CADDIS
(SPECKLED PETER)
Family: Helicopsychidae

Helicopsyche borealis—Peak: June—early July.

This caddis hatches from June to early July, in the evening, from all types of trout streams.

HOOK #20 (males one size smaller).

OVERALL LENGTH 7 millimeters.

BODY Bright amber.

WINGS Dark gray.

LEGS Gray.

ANTENNAE Black with light gray rings.

Range: W, NW.

Habitat: Trout streams.

Emergence: Near banks.

Egg laying: On the surface near banks.

36

Tiny Black Caddis
(Speckled Peter)

ADULT IMITATION

WINGS Dark gray hackle feathers.

BODY Bright amber dubbing.

HACKLE Gray.

ANTENNAE Black hackle stems, stripped.

Adult imitation

This is an important species because its emergence is concentrated, even though it is a small insect and often overlooked by fishermen. It emerges from mid-June to early July in the Rocky Mountain West, and early May to June on the Pacific Coast. This species prefers moderate currents rather than fast riffles. Emergence is in the evening in open water. Egg laying is also in the evening. The females either flop on the water when releasing their egg balls, or they crawl underwater from overhanging grasses, swim to the bottom, release the egg mass, and swim back to the surface. In either case, after ovipositing they ride the water in the normal resting position, drifting close to the bank, where trout unhurriedly sip them. The egg-laying flight is more important than the emergence. Even though these insects are small, they often emerge in numbers that can overshadow much larger insects like the green drake mayfly.

Green Sedge
(Green Rock Worm)

Rhyacophila coloradensis

Adult *Rhyacophila* (above and below)

GREEN SEDGE
(GREEN ROCK WORM)
Family: Rhyacophilidae

Rhyacophila bifila, R. coloradensis

Peak: Sporadic; spring to fall.

These caddis hatch spring to fall, in the evening, from fast, cold trout streams.

HOOK #14 (males one size smaller).

OVERALL LENGTH 12–15 millimeters.

BODY Green.

WINGS Grayish brown, mottled.

LEGS Tan.

ANTENNAE Tan with darker bands.

Range: W, NW.

Habitat: Cold-water riffles.

Emergence: Afternoon, from riffles.

Egg laying: Crawls or swims to the bottom in riffles.

Green Sedge
(Green Rock Worm)

ADULT IMITATION

WINGS Mottled bobwhite, grouse, or partridge body feathers.

BODY Green dubbing.

HACKLE Tan.

ANTENNAE Tan hackle stems, stripped.

This is an important genus for trout fishermen, but the larva, known as the green rock worm, is usually more important than the adult, especially to steelhead anglers. The larva is free-living in that it does not build a protective case, so it is unusually vulnerable to predation. In most areas of the West the emergence is not well organized. The worms live in fast pocket water, and the adults emerge and oviposit in the same areas. In situations in which trout are feeding on adults, those adults are usually egg-laying females. Some females ride the water quietly, some hop around, and some crawl underwater, so you will see both splashy and quiet riseforms. Fish will take wet and dry imitations. The adults seem to oviposit mainly on days with very little wind.

The green rock worm. Note the one hard plate behind the head—a characteristic of the *Rhyacophila*.

Adult imitation

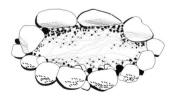

Temporary pupal case

39

Lepidostoma Adult

Lepidostoma case

LITTLE BROWN SEDGE
Family: Lepidostomatidae

Lepidostoma pluviale—Peak: Sporadic; mid-June—early September.

This caddis hatches from mid-June to early September, in the evening.

HOOK #18 (males one size smaller).

OVERALL LENGTH 10 millimeters.

BODY Bright olive.

WINGS Light brown. Males have a distinctive dark gray recurve on the leading edge of the wing, which can be used for identification.

LEGS Brown.

ANTENNAE Brown with lighter rings.

Lepidostoma case: This case is similar to the chimney cases of *Brachycentrus,* but its particles are wider.

Range: W, NW.

Habitat: Widespread.

Emergence: Evening, midstream.

Egg laying: On the surface, afternoon to evening.

Little Brown Sedge

ADULT IMITATION

WINGS Light brown hen feathers.

BODY Olive dubbing.

HACKLE Brown.

ANTENNAE Brown hackle stems, stripped.

Adult imitation

This is an important species because it is widespread and has a long emergence period. It emerges from mid-June to early September in numbers only slightly smaller than those of the cinnamon sedge. Both the emergence and the egg-laying stages are important to the angler. After their evening emergence the adults ride the water for a relatively long time—10 to 20 seconds. Pupal, emerger, and adult patterns all take fish, but the pupal pattern seems to be most effective during the emergence. Both males and females ride the water in the resting position during egg laying, which occurs in the afternoon and evening.

GRAY-WINGED LONG-HORN SEDGE
Family: Leptoceridae

Oecetis disjuncta—Peak: June.

This caddis hatches from early June to late July, during warm summer afternoons and evenings, in all types of trout streams.

HOOK #16 (males one size smaller).

OVERALL LENGTH 10–12 millimeters.

BODY Female—bright golden yellow; male—bright green.

WINGS Light gray. Long and slender.

LEGS Tan.

ANTENNAE Ginger with black rings; more than twice the body length.

Range: W, NW.

Habitat: Slow water.

Emergence: Late afternoon or evening in midstream.

Egg laying: On the surface.

Adult *Oecetis disjuncta*

Oecetis case

Gray-Winged Long-Horn Sedge

ADULT IMITATION

WINGS Light gray hen body feather, long and slender. (The wings are approximately 1.5 times the length of the body—longer than those of most caddisflies, which average about 1.25 times body length.)

BODY Bright green or yellow dubbing.

HACKLE Tan.

ANTENNAE Tan hackle stems, stripped, very long.

Adult imitation

This is an important species because its members hatch in the late spring and summer in the West and are large insects, which the trout seem to relish even when the peak emergence is over. They are on the wing when pale morning duns and green drakes are emerging and many anglers are at the river. These insects produce good rises, but anglers often overlook them to concentrate on the more popular mayflies. The fish often prefer the caddisflies.

Egg laying is the most important stage, but fish will feed on the emergers. Both emergence and ovipositing occur in late afternoon and evening. Both adults and spent imitations fished dead drift are effective. Medium to slow currents produce the larger hatches.

NOTE: The closely related tan-winged long-horn sedge *(Oecetis avara)* is less important, but can overlap the hatch of the gray-winged. Its behavior is similar; #16.

43

Black Dancer
(Black Long-Horn Sedge)

Adult *Mystacides*

Mystacides case

BLACK DANCER (BLACK LONG-HORN SEDGE)
Family: Leptoceridae

Mystacides alafimbriata—Peak: August.

This caddis hatches from late July to late August in slow water, morning and evening.

HOOK #18 (males one size smaller).

OVERALL LENGTH 9 millimeters.

BODY Black to dull amber.

WINGS Red-brown to black. Long and slender.

LEGS Brown or dark gray.

ANTENNAE Black with light gray rings; more than twice the body length.

Range: W, NW.

Habitat: Slow water.

Emergence: Morning, midstream.

Egg laying: Evening, midstream and near banks.

Black Dancer
(Black Long-Horn Sedge)

Adult Imitation

WINGS Black or brown hen hackle feathers, long and slender. (The wings are approximately 1.5 times the length of the body—longer than those of most caddisflies, which average about 1.25 times body length.)

BODY Black or amber dubbing.

HACKLE Black.

ANTENNAE Black hackle stems, stripped, very long.

Adult imitation

This is an important species because its peak emergence in the West is in August, when insect activity is much lighter than in June and July. The caddis emerge in the morning from 7 to 10, when the temperature is cool and pleasant. Ovipositing is in the evening.

This fly rides the water serenely in a resting position for long distances. Trout take it quietly. Adult patterns are all you need, although trout will take the pupa at times.

GREAT GRAY-SPOTTED SEDGE
Family: Hydropsychidae

Arctopsyche grandis—Peak: Late June–July.

HOOK #8 (males one size smaller).

OVERALL LENGTH 17–20 millimeters.

BODY Olive.

WINGS Grayish brown with light brown speckles.

LEGS Brown.

ANTENNAE Brown with darker rings.

Range: W.

Habitat: Trout rivers.

Emergence: Mainly at night.

Egg laying: Mainly at night.

Adult *Arctopsyche Grandis*

Arctopsyche larva

Great Gray-Spotted Sedge

ADULT IMITATION

WINGS Brown.

BODY Olive.

HACKLE Brown.

ANTENNAE Brown.

The larval stage is by far the most important and can be used as a searching pattern during warm months. This caddis mainly emerges and lays eggs at night, which could be of interest to night fishermen.

Adult imitation

Great Silver-Striped Sedge
(Giant Golden Caddis)

GREAT SILVER-STRIPED SEDGE (GIANT GOLDEN CADDIS)
Family: Limnephilidae

Adult *Hesperophylax*

Hesperophylax designatus—Peak: Early July.

HOOK #8 (males one size smaller).

OVERALL LENGTH 17–20 millimeters.

BODY Bright olive.

WINGS Light ginger, with a silver stripe.

LEGS Ginger.

ANTENNAE Ginger.

Range: W.

Habitat: Trout rivers.

Emergence: Night.

Egg laying: Daytime.

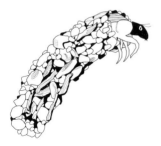

Hesperophylax case

Great Silver-Striped Sedge
(Giant Golden Caddis)

ADULT IMITATION

WINGS Light ginger, silver striped.

BODY Bright olive.

HACKLE Ginger.

ANTENNAE Ginger.

The ovipositing stage of this species is significant to anglers. The females lay eggs close to banks, often skittering on the surface.

Adult imitation

Giant Orange Sedge
(October Caddis)

Adult *Dicosmoecus*

Dicosmoecus case

GIANT ORANGE SEDGE
(OCTOBER CADDIS)
Family: Limnephilidae

*Dicosmoecus atripes, D. gilvipes,
D. jucundus*

Peak: September–October.

HOOK #4–8.

OVERALL LENGTH 20–28 millimeters.

BODY Orange.

WINGS Gray with slight mottling.

LEGS Tan.

ANTENNAE Tan.

Range: W, NW.

Habitat: Moderate to fast water.

Emergence: In shallows, evening.

Egg laying: At dusk, on the surface.

Giant Orange Sedge
(October Caddis)

ADULT IMITATION

WINGS Gray hen body feather.

BODY Orange dubbing.

HACKLE Tan.

ANTENNAE Brown hackle stems, stripped.

Adult imitation

This is a most important genus for trout fishermen in the Pacific Northwest and Rocky Mountains. Every stage of this huge insect is taken by trout, and imitations of each stage are productive. The larvae exhibit behavioral drift in the summer, and unlike most aquatic insects this drift is in the daytime, so they are unusually vulnerable to predation.

The pupae migrate to the shallows in the fall before emerging in the late afternoon and evening. Ovipositing takes place at dusk and the females make quite a commotion, which attracts the attention of very large trout. Fishing a dry adult imitation with a pupa on a dropper in the shallows with a twitching retrieve can be very productive.

The Missouri River below Holter Dam has a good hatch of these caddisflies in September. Even during afternoons when only a few of these Trichoptera are flying, you can hear explosive rises. Trout in this river are on the lookout for these big flies, so the emergence does not need huge numbers of insects for you to enjoy very good angling.

Trout Lake Caddis

Lakes in which trout live must, obviously, provide food for those trout. Most of us think of damselflies, *Callibaetis* mayflies, midges, and scuds as primary sources of food. But caddisflies are also common in such lakes.

As it happens, the lakes that support trout are more common in the western United States and Canada than the East, probably because the high altitudes and latitudes here create the necessary low temperatures.

What we know about stillwater caddis has come primarily from entomologist Rick Hafele, who lives in Oregon and is also a serious angler. His observations are passed on here, partly from an article in *American Angler* magazine.

First, he tells us that caddisflies are better adapted to stillwater environments than are most mayflies or stoneflies. He points out that caddis living in lakes need the means to gather oxygen, since there is no current to bring it to them. Such caddis undulate their abdomens inside their cases to provide water flow over their gills, giving them a supply of oxygen.

There are three families of caddis that are best suited for living in lakes: the *Limnephilidae*, the *Leptoceridae*, and the *Phryganeidae*.

Trout Lake Caddis

TRAVELING SEDGE

The hatch Rick finds most exciting is that of the *Banksiola crotchi*, of the family Phryganeidae. These are called traveling sedges, because they run across the surface to reach shore after emerging. The pupae swim up through open water to reach the lake's surface and shed their pupal shucks; then the adults run across the surface, leaving small wakes. Trout go crazy.

HOOK #8, 2XL.

BODY COLOR Dark olive.

WING COLOR Mottled gray.

PEAK Mid-June—mid-July.

Phryganeidae larva and case

Phryganeidae adult

Trout Lake Caddis

TAN CADDIS
(to distinguish from
the *Hydropsyche*
cinnamon caddis)

Regarding the *Limnephilidae*, Rick says that a few skitter across the surface at emergence, but most fly off the water. Both pupae and adults are taken readily by trout. The genus *Limnephilus*, which includes many species, is the most important of this family.

HOOK #12.

BODY COLOR Tan.

WING COLOR Mottled cinnamon.

Limnephilidae larva

Limnephilidae adult

BLACK DANCER

Leptoceridae are interesting to Rick because the larvae of most species swim (and are eaten) in their cases, using their hind legs for propulsion. Evening is the normal time for species such as *Mystacides sepulchralis* to lay their eggs, by diving underwater. This is a close relative of the common black dancer known on western trout streams.

Rick says the black dancers are active in shallow water, in large numbers, both as emergers and egg layers. The *Leptoceridae* tend to be gray to shiny black, and are found in sizes 16 to 12. This entire family is noted by its designation as long-horn sedges.

Leptoceridae larva

HOOK #14.

BODY COLOR Dark gray.

WING COLOR Shiny black.

ANTENNAE Long ginger.

Leptoceridae adult

Trout Lake Caddis

The chart Rick published listing the genera and species is reproduced here.

FAMILY	GENUS	SPECIES	LOCATION
Limnephilidae	Clistoronia	magnifica	NW, W, Can
"	Asynarchus	montanus	W, Can
"	Grammotaulius	lorettae	W, Can
"	Lenarchus	vastus	N, W, Can
"	Limnephilus	90+	All regions
"	Nemotaulius	hostilis	N, Can
"	Onocosmoecus	quadrinotatus	E
"	Platycentropus	radiatus	E
Leptoceridae	Mystacides	sepulchralis	All regions
"	Nectopsyche	albida	"
"	Oecetis	inconspicua	"
"	Trianodes	25+	"
Phryganeidae	Agrypnia	pagetana	N, Can
"	Banksiola	crotchi	All regions
"	Banksiola	dossuaria	N, E
"	Fabria	inornata	N, E
"	Ptilostomis	ocellifera	All regions

These families of caddis are suited to stillwater environments. Therefore, they should help answer several questions that we plan to research:

- Where do we find the cases of these insects in the lakes?

- Which species are the most important in lakes outside the western United States and Canada?

- Which are found to inhabit warm-water lakes, thus feeding such fish as bass and sunfish?

Chapter 5

MAJOR HATCHES
EAST OF THE MISSISSIPPI

The hatch dates listed in this section are generally for New York through Michigan. In more southerly latitudes flies will hatch earlier; in more northerly latitudes, later.

As in the western chapter, the most important flies are color-coded—red, blue, and yellow—in order of importance. The hatches shown are roughly chronological, in the order of their peaks.

Black Caddis

Brachycentrus lateralis

Brachycentrus americanus

B. lateralis case   B. numerosus case

BLACK CADDIS
Family: Brachycentridae

Brachycentrus lateralis, B. numerosus, B. appalachia, B. solomoni—Peak: Early April–mid-June.

These flies emerge in April and May, at midday, from cold-water trout streams and cold tailwaters. Their characteristics are:

HOOK #16 (males one size smaller).

OVERALL LENGTH 9–13 millimeters.

BODY Dark gray with green or tan lateral line.

WINGS Gray.

LEGS Gray.

ANTENNAE Dark gray with lighter rings.

NOTE: *B. americanus* has a brownish cast and is larger than *B. lateralis*.

Brachycentrus case: The case of the little black caddis is known as a chimney case. It has a square cross section and is tapered. The cases can be found clinging to stones and wood, and they are numerous before the hatch. (The *B. numerosus* case is tubular at the bottom, and only square at the top.) When checking cases, be sure to note whether they contain larvae or not, because empty cases last quite a while and their presence can be misleading.

Range: NE, SE, M.

Black Caddis

Habitat: Cold trout streams.

Emergence: Midday, midstream.

Egg laying: Midday and afternoon, midstream.

The pupae often drift many feet attached to the surface film before emerging.

ADULT IMITATION

WINGS Gray hen hackles.

BODY Dark gray dubbing.

HACKLE Gray.

ANTENNAE Dark gray hackle stem, stripped.

This is the year's first heavy emergence of caddisflies in the East, and trout feed heavily on it. The hatch usually occurs on undammed trout streams and bottom-release tailwaters. The flies begin emerging around midday, just as the hendrickson hatch is waning. Egg laying is in the afternoon and can coincide with the emergence. Peak emergence occurs from the last half of April to mid-June, on balmy days. The adults drift up to 30 feet struggling from their pupal shucks. Once out, they may drift on the surface or fly away quickly. They oviposit much like mayflies, dipping their bodies onto the surface, although some individuals may crawl or dive underwater.

B. americanus case

Brachycentrus pupa

Adult *Ceratopsyche*

CINNAMON CADDIS
Family: Hydropsychidae

Ceratopsyche bifida, C. sparna, C. slossonae, et al.

Peak: All season.

These flies emerge from May to September, mainly in the evening in summer, but some earlier in the day. They are most important in tailwaters, but some are found in trout streams. Their characteristics are:

HOOK #16 (males one size smaller).

OVERALL LENGTH 9–15 millimeters.

BODY Cinnamon brown.

WINGS Brownish gray with a speckling of small tan spots.

LEGS Brown.

ANTENNAE Tan with dark rings.

Ceratopsyche larva: This larva is characterized by three hard, dark plates on the body segments behind its head, as are its relatives in the family Hydropsychidae. Bodies are tan or gray.

It builds a net like a spiderweb among the gravel to trap food. It does not build a case until it is ready to pupate, about two weeks before emergence.

Range: NE, SE, M.

Cinnamon Caddis

Habitat: Mainly tailwaters, but also widespread.

Emergence: Morning, afternoon, and evening, midstream.

Egg laying: Morning and evening; swimming or crawling underwater.

The pupa often drifts many feet attached to the surface film before emerging.

ADULT IMITATION

WINGS Mottled tan and gray-brown grouse or quail body feathers.

BODY Cinnamon dubbing.

HACKLE Brown.

ANTENNAE Dark brown hackle stem, stripped.

This is by far the most important family for trout fishermen. Only in the early spring when little black caddis and tiny black caddis are on the water do any other caddisflies even come close in importance to this fly and its cousin, the little olive caddis.

Adult imitation

Cinnamon Caddis

They hatch in large numbers, usually in the evening but also in the morning, seemingly when the nights are very warm. Egg laying is done in the morning and evening, with some during the day.

These caddisflies drift as pupae for a long time before their emergence. They also take a long time to struggle from their pupal shucks. These two factors allow you to hook a lot of fish long before the hatch begins on a pupal imitation fished dead drift on the bottom, as a floating pupa just under the surface film, or as an emerger. The pupae emerge in midstream.

The females crawl or dive underwater or sprawl on the surface to lay eggs. A surface-fished dry fly is often effective during egg laying, or it can be pulled under the surface to imitate the returning egg-laying female.

Many spent caddis collect on the water after dark, and the fish will feed selectively on quad-wing patterns at that time.

Cinnamon Caddis

To find out which stage of the insect the fish are taking, tie on a floating fly, tie a dropper from it, and attach a pupal imitation, which will float just under the surface. Fish these dead drift. If the fish take one consistently you know which fly to use.

If the fish rise all around your flies but do not take, pull the dry fly underwater. It may then be taken for an egg-laying female returning to the surface.

At the end of egg laying, fish will often take a spent imitation. A quad-wing fly or delta-wing fly will then work.

NOTE: Those caddisflies that do not live in cases as larvae—such as this one—build cases briefly for a couple of weeks to change into pupae. You can easily tell one of these pupal cases from the normal larval case because it is open on one side. When you take a knife and remove it from a rock, the entire pupa, enclosed in a silk sac, is exposed as if in a window (see illustration).

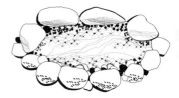

Temporary case

Little Olive Caddis
(Little Sister Sedge)

Cheumatopsyche adult

LITTLE OLIVE CADDIS
(LITTLE SISTER SEDGE)
Family: Hydropsychidae

Cheumatopsyche speciosa, C. pettiti, C. lasia, C. campyla, C. harwoodi

Peak: All season.

These flies emerge from May to September, mainly during the evening in summer, but some earlier in the day (in September, they emerge in the morning). They are most important in tailwaters, but some are found in trout streams. Their characteristics are:

HOOK #18 (males one size smaller).

OVERALL LENGTH 7.5 millimeters.

BODY Olive.

WINGS Brownish gray with a speckling of small tan markings.

LEGS Brown.

ANTENNAE Tan with dark rings.

Little Olive Caddis
(Little Sister Sedge)

Cheumatopsyche larva: This larva is characterized by three dark plates on the body segments behind the head, as are its relatives in the family Hydropsychidae. Bodies are green to olive.

It builds a net like a spiderweb among the gravel to trap food. It does not build a case until it is ready to pupate, about two weeks before emergence.

Range: NE, SE, M.

Habitat: Riffles in warm tailwaters.

Emergence: Afternoon and evening in midstream.

Egg laying: Swims or crawls underwater.

The pupa often drifts many feet just under the surface film before emerging.

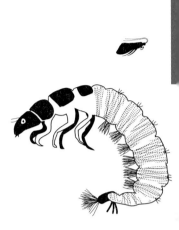

Cheumatopsyche larva

ADULT IMITATION

WINGS Mottled tan and gray-brown grouse or quail body feathers.

BODY Olive.

Temporary case

HACKLE Brown.

ANTENNAE Dark brown hackle stem, stripped.

Little Olive Caddis
(Little Sister Sedge)

Adult imitation in summer colors

This is the second most important genus for trout fishermen, a close second to *Hydropsyche/Ceratopsyche*, to which it is closely related. Since these genera belong to the same family their habits, style of emergence, and egg laying are very similar, if not identical. They hatch and lay eggs at the same time of day, interspersed with the cinnamon caddis hatch.

These insects are similar in shape to cinnamon caddis and have the same unique wing shape. They are a little smaller than *Ceratopsyche* and can easily be distinguished from them by their smaller size and olive body color. The few *Ceratopsyche* that have olive bodies at emergence (which quickly turn cinnamon or brown) are larger. These caddisflies become much lighter as the season progresses—as do many other species, but the little olive seems to exhibit this trait in the extreme. The wings, which are dark in the early season, become much lighter in fall and appear white in flight. They are usually evening emergers in the summer, but some switch to morning emergence in the fall.

Little Olive Caddis
(Little Sister Sedge)

The females dive underwater or sprawl on the surface to lay eggs. A surface-fished dry fly is often effective during egg laying, or it can be pulled under the surface to imitate the returning egg-laying female.

Many spent caddis collect on the water after dark, and the fish will feed selectively on quad-wing patterns at that time.

Adult imitation in fall colors

Dark Blue Sedge

Psilotreta frontalis

Psilotreta case

DARK BLUE SEDGE
(East and Appalachia only)
Family: Odontoceridae

Psilotreta labida, P. frontalis—Peak: Late April–mid-June.

These flies emerge from late April to mid-June, in the evening, on all types of trout streams. Their characteristics are:

HOOK #14 (males one size smaller).

OVERALL LENGTH 12–15 millimeters.

BODY Green to almost black.

WINGS Dark grayish brown with small light spots.

LEGS Very dark gray.

ANTENNAE Black.

Range: NE, SE.

Habitat: On rocks in moderate riffles.

Emergence: Evening.

Egg laying: On the surface, in the evening.

Dark Blue Sedge

Adult Imitation

WINGS Dark gray hen hackles.

BODY Black to dark green.

HACKLE Very dark gray.

ANTENNAE Black.

These are important species in the East and mid-South from late April to June. They emerge in the evening. The pupae swim to the surface to emerge, and females flop on the surface to oviposit, both in the evening. Trout are attracted to this commotion, and dry imitations work best.

Adult imitation

Green Sedge
(Green Rock Worm)

Rhyacophila melita

GREEN SEDGE (GREEN ROCK WORM)
Family: Rhyacophilidae

Rhyacophila fuscula (East)
R. melita, R. manistee (Midwest)
R. fuscula, R. vuphipes (South)

Peak: Sporadic; spring to fall.

These caddis hatch spring to fall in the evening from fast, cold trout streams.

HOOK #14 (males one size smaller).

OVERALL LENGTH 12–15 millimeters, a few species to 18 millimeters.

BODY Green.

WINGS Grayish brown, mottled.

LEGS Tan.

ANTENNAE Tan with darker bands.

Range: NE, SE, M.

Habitat: Cold-water riffles.

Emergence: Afternoon, from riffles.

Egg laying: Crawls or swims to the bottom in riffles.

Green rock worms are free-living larvae that do not build cases, except briefly before emerging. Each has one hard plate behind its head.

Green Sedge
(Green Rock Worm)

ADULT IMITATION

WINGS Mottled bobwhite, grouse, or partridge body feathers.

BODY Green dubbing.

HACKLE Tan.

ANTENNAE Tan hackle stems, stripped.

Adult imitation

This is an important genus for trout fishermen, but the larva, known as the green rock worm, is usually more important than the adult. The larva is free-living in that it does not build a protective case, so it is unusually vulnerable to predation. In most areas emergence is not heavily concentrated. The worms live in fast pocket water, and the adults emerge and oviposit in the same areas. In situations in which trout are feeding on adults, those adults are usually egg-laying females. Some females ride the water quietly, some hop around, and some crawl underwater, so you will see both splashy and quiet riseforms. Fish will take wet and dry imitations. The adults seem to oviposit mainly on days with very little wind.

Tiny Black Caddis
(Short-Horn Sedge)

Adult *Glossosoma*

Glossosoma case

TINY BLACK CADDIS
(SHORT-HORN SEDGE)
Family: Glossosomatidae

Glossosoma nigrior—Peak: Spring mornings.

These flies emerge sporadically from spring to fall in trout streams, occasionally in large numbers, usually in the morning.

HOOK #20 (males one size smaller).

OVERALL LENGTH 6–7.5 millimeters.

BODY Black.

WINGS Black with a few light tan spots midwing, and a few at the wing tips.

LEGS Dark gray.

ANTENNAE Black.

Glossosoma case: This case is known as a domed saddle case. The larva takes the case with it as it moves along the surface of rocks.

Range: NE, M.

Habitat: Cold streams.

Emergence: Riffles in midstream, crawling to the banks.

Egg laying: Submerges in riffles.

Tiny Black Caddis
(Short-Horn Sedge)

ADULT IMITATION

WINGS Black hen hackle.

BODY Black dubbing.

HACKLE Gray.

ANTENNAE Black hackle stems, stripped.

This is an important species because its members emerge all season long, usually a few at a time but occasionally in good numbers. They can cause heavy feeding when the emergence is large, and some rises when the hatch is light. Since these are small, dark forms, they are hard to see, but fish will feed on them. (You may notice that the trout are rising, but see nothing on the water.) The most important time for this hatch is during spring mornings, because not much else is emerging at this time.

Adult imitation

The pupae emerge in midstream, and pupal and emerger imitations are effective. In the spring some pupae emerge in midstream and crawl on the surface of the water to shore. A hackled pupal imitation skittered on the surface is very effective at these times. Females submerge to oviposit.

Microsema rusticum

TINY BLACK CADDIS
Family: Brachycentridae

Micrasema scotti (E & S)
M. rusticum (M)

Peak: April–mid-May; September–October.

HOOK #20 (males one size smaller).

OVERALL LENGTH 7–9 millimeters.

BODY Dark gray with green or tan lateral line.

WINGS Black.

LEGS Dark gray.

ANTENNAE Dark gray with lighter rings.

Range: NE, SE, M.

Habitat: Cold streams.

Emergence: Morning and evening.

Egg laying: Morning and evening.

Micrasema case

Tiny Black Caddis

Adult Imitation

WINGS Dark gray hen hackle.

BODY Dark gray dubbing.

HACKLE Gray.

ANTENNAE Dark gray hackle stems, stripped.

These are important species because the peak emergence in the East and Midwest is concentrated. Although hard to see, the insects hatch in large numbers to emerge and oviposit during mornings and evenings. These insects ride the water for only a very short time, so pupal patterns are much more effective than emergers or adults.

Adult imitation

Females lay their eggs on the river bottom. They then swim back to the surface, floating awash in the film, where spentwing imitations are the most effective, fished dry. Adult imitations are effective fished wet. Some individuals may dip their eggs on the surface.

On some very cold tailwaters, such as the South Holston of Tennessee, there are spring and fall emergences of *M. scotti.*

Zebra Caddis

ZEBRA CADDIS
Family: Hydropsychidae

Macrostemum zebratum—Peak: Mid-summer evenings.

HOOK #12 (males one size smaller).

OVERALL LENGTH 15–18 millimeters.

BODY Freshly emerged—green, black ribbing; later—black body, yellow ribbing.

WINGS Ginger, black markings as shown.

LEGS Yellow.

ANTENNAE Very long, black.

Range: NE, SE, M.

Habitat: Warm trout rivers.

Emergence: Warm summer evenings.

Egg laying: Dives or sprawls in the evening and after dark.

Adult *Macrostemum*

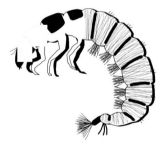

Macrostemum larva

Zebra Caddis

ADULT IMITATION

WINGS Ginger with black stripes.

BODY Freshly emerged—fat green body, black ribbing; later—black dubbing, yellow ribbing.

HACKLE Ginger.

ANTENNAE Black.

This is an important caddisfly in the East, Midwest, and Southeast because it is a large insect, its emergence and egg-laying flights are often huge, and it appears during warm summer evenings when many anglers are fishing. These insects are not found on very cold trout streams, but most of our warmer rivers, like the Housatonic in Connecticut and the Muskegon in Michigan, have large hatches. When these insects are on the water trout will not refuse a well-tied imitation. Some females crawl underwater to oviposit; others dive from high in the air, hit the water, and either sprawl on the surface or actually dive underwater to oviposit. It has been written that many species of caddisflies dive underwater for egg laying, but this is one of the few species we have actually observed doing so.

The larvae are fat and meaty and, since they are net builders, they are available for predation. An imitation of this stage, fished on the bottom, is a good searching pattern in the spring and summer.

Adult imitation

77

Tan-Winged Long-Horn Sedge

TAN-WINGED LONG-HORN SEDGE
Family: Leptoceridae

Adult *Oecetis*

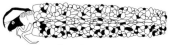

Oecetis case

Oecetis avara—Peak: Warm summer evenings.

This caddis hatches from late May to September during warm summer evenings, in all types of trout streams.

HOOK #16.

OVERALL LENGTH 10–12 millimeters.

BODY Female—dull yellow; male—olive.

WINGS Tan. Long and slender.

LEGS Ginger.

ANTENNAE Ginger, with dark bands; more than twice the body length.

Range: NE, SE, M.

Habitat: Slow water.

Emergence: Warm summer afternoons and evenings, edges and slow water.

Egg laying: On the surface and edges, in slow water.

Tan-Winged Long-Horn Sedge

ADULT IMITATION

WINGS Tan hen hackle, long and slender. (The wings are approximately 1.5 times the length of the body— longer than those of most caddisflies, which average about 1.25 times body length.)

BODY Olive or dull yellow dubbing.

HACKLE Tan.

ANTENNAE Tan hackle stems, stripped, very long.

Adult imitation

This is an important species because its members fly almost all summer on warm evenings, are fairly large, and can emerge in huge numbers. Like all the species in this family, they have antennae 2.5 times the length of their bodies. The pupae swim to the surface to emerge, and the adults sprawl on the surface or dive underwater to oviposit. Emergence is during warm afternoons and evenings. When trout feed on this species they generally take adults on the surface, although they do take pupae as well.

NOTE: The closely related brown long-horn sedge *(Oecetis inconspicua)* is less important, but can overlap the hatch of the tan-winged. Its behavior is similar; #16.

Dark Long-Horn Sedge

DARK LONG-HORN SEDGE
Family: Leptoceridae

Ceraclea transversa—Peak: Midsummer evenings, after dark.

HOOK #16 (males one size smaller).

OVERALL LENGTH 11–16 millimeters.

BODY Dark red-brown to black.

WINGS Red-brown to brownish gray, often with pale markings.

LEGS Brown or dark gray.

ANTENNAE Brown to black; more than twice the body length.

Range: NE, SE, M.

Habitat: Widespread.

Emergence: Warm summer evenings, midstream.

Egg laying: On the surface, or swimming to the bottom.

Adult *Ceraclea*

Ceraclea case

Dark Long-Horn Sedge

ADULT IMITATION

WINGS Black or brown hen hackle feathers, long and slender. (The wings are approximately 1.5 times the length of the body—longer than those of most caddisflies, which average about 1.25 times body length.)

BODY Red-brown or black dubbing.

HACKLE Brown or black.

ANTENNAE Brown hackle stems, stripped, very long.

This is an important species because its members fly almost all summer on warm evenings, are fairly large, and can emerge in huge numbers. They have antennae 2.5 times the length of their bodies. The pupae swim to the surface to emerge, and the adults sprawl on the surface or dive underwater to oviposit. Emergence is during warm evenings and after dark. When trout feed on this species they generally take adults on the surface, although they do take the pupae as well.

White Miller
(White Long-Horn Sedge)

Nectopsyche Adult

Nectopsyche case

WHITE MILLER (WHITE LONG-HORN SEDGE)
Family: Leptoceridae

Nectopsyche albida, N. exquisita

Peak: Evening; August–September.

HOOK #16 (males one size larger).

OVERALL LENGTH 10–11 millimeters.

BODY Light olive.

WINGS Cream. Long and slender.

LEGS Ginger.

ANTENNAE White with tan rings; more than twice the body length.

Range: NE, SE, M.

Habitat: Riffles, slow water.

Emergence: Midstream, at and after dark.

Egg laying: Riffles, in the evening.

White Miller
(White Long-Horn Sedge)

ADULT IMITATION

WINGS Cream hen hackle feathers, long and slender. (The wings are approximately 1.5 times the length of the body—longer than those of most caddisflies, which average about 1.25 times body length.)

BODY Light olive with ginger thorax.

HACKLE Ginger.

ANTENNAE Cream hackle stems, stripped, very long.

Adult imitation

These are important species because they fly midsummer to fall on warm evenings, are fairly large, and can emerge in huge numbers. Due to its color, the white miller is a conspicuous insect. It emerges in the evening and after dusk in large numbers. Both the emergence and the egg-laying stages are important to the angler. The pupae swim to the surface to emerge. Females submerge or sprawl on the surface to oviposit in late evening and after dark.

Dot-Winged Sedge

Adult *Frenesia*

Frenesia case

DOT-WINGED SEDGE

Large Dot-Winged Sedge
Family: Limnephilidae

Frenesia missa, F. difficilis—Peak:
October, in the East.

Small Dot-Winged Sedge
Family: Uenoidae

Neophylax fuscus—Peak: September–
October, in the Midwest.

LARGE DOT-WINGED SEDGE

HOOK #16 (males one size smaller).

OVERALL LENGTH *F. missa*—12 millimeters; *F. difficilis*—15 millimeters.

BODY Dark gray with light tan lateral
line.

WINGS Dark brown with many small,
light tan dots.

LEGS Brownish yellow.

ANTENNAE Brownish yellow and
white with tan rings.

SMALL DOT-WINGED SEDGE

HOOK #18 (males one size smaller).

OVERALL LENGTH 11 millimeters.

Dot-Winged Sedge

Range: NE, M.

Emergence: In the shallows, daytime.

Egg laying: Near shore.

ADULT IMITATION

WINGS Dark brown hen hackle feathers. The wings should be long in relation to the body.

BODY Dark gray with ginger thorax.

HACKLE Ginger.

ANTENNAE Ginger.

Neophylax case

These are important species for fall trout fishermen. The pupae emerge in the daytime by crawling to the shallows to hatch. Pupal imitations fished slow and deep are effective, as are adults fished dry. Adults oviposit near shore. Because adult imitations are so effective, it is possible that some females submerge to oviposit.

These insects can come in large numbers, especially on warm, sunny fall days, and since not much else is emerging at this time, fish feed voraciously on them.

N. fuscus is a common and important fall caddisfly in the Midwest. It looks very much like a Brachycentridae in the hand, but the only genus of Brachycentridae that emerges in the fall is *Micrasema*, which does not have the small light dots on the wings.

Adult imitation

GREAT BROWN AUTUMN SEDGE
Family: Limnephilidae

Pycnopsyche guttifer, P. lepida—Peak: Late August–September.

HOOK #8 (males one size smaller).

OVERALL LENGTH 19–21 millimeters.

BODY Ginger.

WINGS Yellowish brown with two conspicuous black marks.

LEGS Ginger.

ANTENNAE Black.

Range: NE, M.

Habitat: Logs along edges.

Emergence: Mainly at night.

Egg laying: Mainly at night, occasionally afternoon.

Pycnopsyche lepida

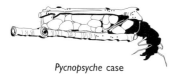

Pycnopsyche case

Great Brown Autumn Sedge

ADULT IMITATION

WINGS Ginger, marked with a black marker.

BODY Ginger dubbing with good flotation.

HACKLE Ginger.

ANTENNAE Black.

The cases of these caddis can be easily spotted by looking on logs around the edge of the stream. The insects are nighttime emergers, with occasional activity at first light or in the afternoon.

You can often see large numbers flying around grassy areas near trout streams on sunny afternoons in the fall. They are so large that when we first noticed them, we thought they were butterflies.

Adult imitation

Chapter 6

TYING CADDIS IMITATIONS

Because the behavior of the caddisflies is complex, tying effective imitations of them requires using some different forms.

Any fly pattern is subject to infinite variation and creativity, of course, so go to it at your tying bench and experiment on the river. Our objective is to provide one basic, simple pattern for each of the major stages of the caddis.

The hook sizes we refer to are based on the following brands and styles:

Orvis	1523 (Big Eye 1639)
Tiemco	5230
Dai-Riki	305
Mustad	94840

Different tyers might use different sizes of hooks, because of different perceptions of sizes, or different ratios of body length to wing length. The overall length of most caddis adults is 1.4 times the body length (inversely, the body is 0.7 times the overall length). A few variations are mentioned in the text. We have also noted that males are normally one size smaller than females. Since females are on the water more, we usually start our fishing with that size of artificial, but males can be important at hatch time and as spent flies after mating.

The patterns here are based on the cinnamon caddis, the olive caddis, and the black caddis. Most caddis can be imitated with a variation of these three. The individual descriptions of each hatch include depictions of the varying colors you can use for imitation. For color, then, use the pictures and descriptions in the text.

The patterns are listed in order of the life cycle of the caddisfly. First is the free larva.

Since the larva drifts with its head down, it should be imitated with the pattern we call the Beadhead-Down. The fly is tied backward, on a curved caddis hook. The bead is dark, and tied to form the head.

Beadhead-Down Larva

Hook Heavy-wire shrimp/caddis hook, #16.
Body Olive Body Stretch over hare's ear dubbing.
Ribbing Fine copper wire.
Antennae None.
Legs Partridge.
Head Black bead.

Beadhead-Down Larva

This fly should be fished near the bottom with a strike indicator, lifting slightly to give the fly up-and-down motion, but otherwise dead-drifted.

Deep-Drifting Pupa

Hook Heavy-wire shrimp/caddis hook, #16.
Body Ginger Antron dubbing.
Dorsal Ribbing Dark brown marking pen.
Legs Mallard duck flank, dyed brown.
Antennae None.
Wings Dark brown quill.
Head Dark brown Antron dubbing.

Deep-Drifting Pupa

This fly should be fished dead drift along the bottom, then tugged gradually toward the surface with a twitching motion, to give motion to its swimming legs. It should not be tied with a beadhead, which would keep the body from drifting horizontally.

Underdrifting Pupa

Hook Light-wire Orvis Big Eye, 1639, #16.
Body Ginger Antron dubbing.
Legs Mallard flank feathers, dyed brown.
Wings (flotation) Snowshoe rabbit foot.
Rib Krystal Flash.

We have found that using snowshoe rabbit foot in place of a wing floats this fly best. This is for flotation only, and to keep the body just under the surface.

Underdrifting Pupa

This fly should float right under the surface film dead drift, or it may be fished as a dropper behind an emerger or adult pattern. Some people find that this is often as effective as an emerger pattern.

Teardrop Emerger

Hook Light-wire Orvis Big Eye, #16.
Shuck Ginger Z-Lon.
Body Ginger Antron.
Wing Snowshoe rabbit.
Hackle None.

Teardrop Emerger

This is a simplified teardrop emerger pattern. It is usually fished dead drift on the surface, with occasional tiny twitches.

Adult Caddis

Hook Light-wire Orvis Big Eye, #16.
Body Ginger cream Fly Rite.
Wings Mottled tan Fly Film.
Hackle Ginger.
Antennae Tan.

Adult Caddis

This pattern may be tied in many ways. We have found Fly Film or Aire-Flow to be the simplest. The choice depends on the color and pattern. Fly Film is good when a clear or marked wing is called for; Aire-Flow has some good mottled colors. A light dressing

Adult Caddis

of elk hair or coastal deer hair can be tied as an over-wing to add flotation. Taped or coated wings can also be used.

This fly can be fished as a dead-drifting adult, as a returning egg layer—under the surface—or as a skittered fly. Skittering is accomplished by wiggling the rod tip horizontally.

Spentwing Caddis

Hook Light-wire Orvis Big Eye, #16.
Body Ginger cream Fly Rite.
Wings Tan poly yarn.
Legs None.
Antennae Tan.

Spentwing Caddis

This fly is usually fished after dark, dead drift, on calm, flat water. The spent caddis fall to the water after their final egg laying and are easy prey for fish, which feed with extreme selectivity after dark. We have mentioned that at such times it may be necessary to pick the site of the last rise, drift your fly to that spot, then set the hook before seeing a rise.

Chapter 7

MASTER LIST OF CADDIS PATTERNS

This list will cover most of the natural caddisflies you're likely to see on trout streams in numbers that would cause selective feeding by trout. The most important hatches are marked with an asterisk.

Each pattern and size can be tied in an adult, pupa, larva, or spentwing version, as needed.

1. **Black Caddis**	Common hook size
*Brachycentrus**	#16
Micrasema	#20
Amiocentrus	#20
Glossosoma	#20
Mystacides	#16
Ceraclea	#14
Neophylax	#18

Materials:
Body Dark gray dubbing.
Wings Black or gray hen hackle on Scotch tape, cemented, folded, and clipped to shape.

2. **Green Sedge**	
Rhyacophila	#14
*Cheumatopsyche**	#18
Lepidostoma	#16

Materials:
Body Olive green dubbing.
Wings Brown speckled partridge back feathers on Scotch tape, cemented, folded, and clipped to shape.
Hackle Brown.

3. **Cinnamon Caddis**

	Common hook size
*Hydropsyche**	#16
*Ceratopsyche**	#16
Helicopsyche	#20

Materials:
Body Cinnamon dubbing.
Wings Brown speckled partridge back feathers on Scotch tape, cemented, folded, and clipped to shape.
Hackle Light brown.

4. **Tan Long-Horn Sedge**

Oecetis	#16

Materials:
Body Tan and olive; ginger thorax.
Wings Tan hen body feather on Scotch tape, cemented, folded, and clipped to shape (slim).
Hackle Tan.

5. **White Miller**

Nectopsyche	#16

Materials:
Body Olive with tan thorax.
Wings Cream hen body feather on Scotch tape, cemented, folded, and clipped to shape (slim).
Hackle Ginger.

6. **Dark Blue Sedge**

*Psilotreta**	#14

Materials:
Body Dark gray to dark green.
Wings Dark gray hen body feather on Scotch tape, cemented, folded, and clipped to shape.
Hackle Dark gray.

7. **Giant Orange Sedge**   Common hook size
   Dicosmoecus   #4–8

Materials:
Body Orange dubbing.
Wings Gray hen body feather on Scotch tape, cemented, folded, and clipped to shape.
Hackle Rusty brown.

You can see that you need only seven patterns in a few sizes to match all the important flies.

Tying the Tape-and-Feather-Winged Cinnamon Caddis

(A more exact imitation of the natural)

This pattern is effective fished either wet or dry during egg laying. Skittering it on the surface is sometimes deadly—especially if females are swimming back to the surface, bouncing on the surface before flying off to mate again, and returning to the river to lay more eggs. It will catch fish during an emergence, but usually the emerger or pupa is better at that time.

Hook #16–18, 3X, fine wire. Males are one size smaller than females. (This is true of most caddisfly species.) The bodies of caddisflies are shorter than the wings, so an imitation tied on a #16 hook will look like a #14 insect. It is important not to tie these patterns too large.

Body Fine-textured cinnamon dubbing. You'll also want to carry a few in yellow and olive.

Antennae Two stripped hackle quills, deer or moose hair, flank feathers from mallard or wood ducks (optional—they make the fly look a lot better but are fragile). Guard hairs from mink tails and various other animals are the most durable, as well as synthetic fibers.

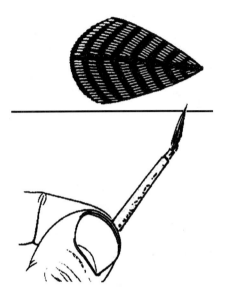

Paint the taped feather with flexible cement.

Wings Back and flank feathers from various birds. Quail, grouse, and plain and variegated hen hackles are ideal for this fly. Press the feathers onto Scotch tape, then coat the feather side with Seal-All, a flexible cement, and let dry. Fold the coated feathers in the middle at the stem to form the wings. Next, clip them to the selected wing shape and tie in.

Thin, clear packaging tape can also be used. This is more flexible than Scotch Tape, so it makes for a softer wing. Alternate wing materials are: coastal deer hair, hackle tips, and poly yarn.

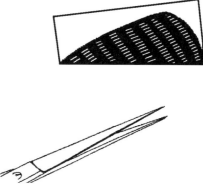

Fold the taped feather in the middle and trim to shape.

The wings of caddisflies have a sheen that hair and feathers do not. This sheen can be added to hair wings by tying a few fibers of Z-Lon or poly yarn under the wing. The cement-coated gamebird feathers get their sheen from the cement and/or the tape. The wings of these insects are lighter than they look when you study them in the hand. If you hold a natural up to the sky and observe it from underneath, you will notice the wings are translucent and appear lighter than when you look at them from the top. This is how the trout see them—from underneath. It is important to use a material that is not too dark.

Hackle Reddish brown hackle tied in before or after the wing, and clipped on top and bottom. Hackle is optional, as the pattern works quite well without it, but it does ensure that the fly lands upright. Hackle can also be tied in parachute-style; such flies are great for skittering. The post for the parachute is round rubber, sold in fly shops. It is tied in on the top of the head and

This is the correct wing shape for all the
cinnamon caddis and little olive caddis.

stretched. We use a gallows tool and hackle pliers to
hold the stretched rubber. After the hackle is wound
around the stretched rubber and tied down, the rubber
post is clipped while still stretched close to the top
of the hackle bunch. The rubber post will pull down
and lock the hackle firmly into place. Doug Swisher
invented this method of tying parachute hackle.

Chapter 8

OCCASIONALLY IMPORTANT CADDISFLIES

Name		Hook Size
Tiny Black Caddis *Chimarra aterrima* Philopotamidae		#20
Black Gold-Spotted Caddis *Dolophilodes distinctus* Philopotamidae		#20
Tiny Dark Eastern Woodland Sedge *Lype diversa* Psychomyiidae		#22
Brown-Checkered Summer Sedge *Polycentropus cinereus* Polycentropodidae		#18
Dinky Purple-Breasted Sedge *Psychomyia flavida* Psychomyiiadae		#22
Giant Cream Pattern-Winged Sedge *Hydatophylax argus* Limnephilidae		#8

Name		Hook Size
Chocolate & Cream Sedge *Platycentropus radiatus* Limnephilidae		#8
Little Gray Sedge *Goera calcarata* Limnephilidae		#18
Summer Flyer, Tan Caddis *Limnephilus sericus,* *L. submonilifer* Limnephilidae		#14
Early Smoky-Winged Sedge *Apatania incerta* Limnephilidae		#20
Dinky Light Summer Sedge *Nyctiophylax moestus* Limnephilidae		#20
Gray-Checkered Sedge *Molanna cinera,* *M. uniophila* Molannidae		#14

FISHERMAN'S SIMPLIFIED KEYS

How to Use this Key

Fly fishermen really should be able to identify caddis-flies to the genus level, because caddisflies are much more difficult to fish than mayflies, for a number of reasons. One of the most important is that many of the most common species crawl underwater to lay their eggs. The females then swim to the surface and fly away. This process can be repeated four or five times. Trout will feed on these ascending females, but trout also feed on ascending pupae during the hatch. You cannot tell if the caddisfly you see flying off the water is a newly emerged insect or an egg-laying female returning to the surface from the bottom and taking wing, because they all look alike. The silhouette of an ascending pupa and an ascending adult are very differ-ent, so to be successful you must be able to discover which stage you're fishing to. The various genera have different habits that will, if known, allow you to be suc-cessful in imitating the actions of the naturals. Some caddisflies crawl underwater to oviposit, some deposit their eggs on the surface, and some deposit their eggs on shore close to water. Some species emerge from the pupal shuck very quickly and some take much longer. Realizing what is going on will be of considerable help.

In our search for a simple, understandable method to identify caddisflies, we first eliminated those families that are not important to anglers. Then we simplified the normal keys and included sizes and colors of the naturals, which most of the scientific keys do not. The result was a key to the families that is simple and easy to use. You should begin by collecting a caddisfly and examining it, noting the total length from the head to the tip of the wing, its color, the shape of the wing, and the length of the antennae. Go to page 109 of the key and start at A. If the insect has antennae that are very long—-more than twice as long as the body—-follow the directions, which say, "go to 1." When you go to 1 you will see you have identified the caddisfly to the family level. As you read the descriptions under 1 you can identify the insect to the genus level and often to the species.

If the insect does *not* have very long antennae, go to B, and so on. Each family identification includes descriptions of the genera in that family and lists the important species. Keys to the most important genera, with their descriptions and habits that are important to fishermen, are found in chapters 4 and 5.

Keys A, B, C, G, H, and I require little or no magnification to identify the insects. Keys D, E, and F require an 8x to 10x slide viewer. Occasionally 20x or 30x would be better when viewing some of the parts (such as ocelli, wing venation, and venters of female caddisflies). Inexpensive magnifying glasses (5x to 50x) can be obtained from BioQuip Products, Inc., 17804 La Salle Avenue, Gardena, CA 90748; (213) 324-0620.

Note: E = East, M = Midwest, AS = Appalachian South, W = West. These letters denote the range of a genus or species. The first word of the common name of a caddisfly denotes its size. **Micro** and **Pseudomicro** = #24–28 (2–5.5 millimeters in length from head to wing tip). **Tiny** = #22–24, **Little** = #20–22, **no size specified** = #6–18, **Great** = #12–14, **Giant** = any size larger than #12. A body on a #16 hook will have #14 wings, because the wings of caddisflies are longer than their bodies.

Classification of Aquatic Insects with a Fisherman's Classification for Caddisflies

Aquatic insects, like other members of the animal kingdom, are classified under categories that are believed to represent the various degrees of relationship displayed by their morphological and other characteristics. One of the most important caddisflies for us, *Ceratopsyche bifida*, is placed in the following categories:

Kingdom: Animal (all animal life)

Subkingdom: Invertebrata (all animals without backbones)

Phylum: Arthropoda (all animals with external skeletons, bilateral symmetry, and jointed legs)

Class: Insecta (all true insects; that is, all arthropods with head, thorax, and abdomen, one pair of antennae, one or two pairs of wings, and three pairs of legs)

Order: Trichoptera (all caddisflies)

Family: Hydropsychidae (all true common net spinners)

Genus: *Ceratopsyche* (a group composed of a few closely related kinds of common net spinners)

Species: *bifida* (a particular kind of common net spinner, capable of interbreeding and producing fertile offspring and normally not interbreeding with other such groups)

Names of families are capitalized and end in *-idae*. Names of genus (the plural is *genera*) are capitalized and printed in italics; names of species are not capitalized and are printed in italics.

A Fisherman's Classification of Caddisflies from Family to Species

You can better understand the importance of the names of the families and genera of caddisflies if we modify the definitions of them. This change is only accurate for caddisfly genera in which all species are usually about the same size and color. It is not accurate for mayflies, where the species in a genus can vary considerably in size and color. The color of the bodies of caddisflies can vary somewhat in a single species even when they are found on the same river.

Family: A group of caddisflies that have the same emerging and egg-laying habits, and similar shapes, but differ in size and color.

Genus: A group of caddisflies in the same family that are usually very similar in size and color.

Species: A group of caddisflies in the same genus that are minutely different in structure. This difference is usually of no importance to fly fishermen or tyers.

An Introduction to the Classification of Caddisflies by the Shape of Their Maxillary Palps and Presence or Absence of Ocelli

Some families can be identified by the naked eye. Some of the most important families require you to examine the anatomy of the maxillary palps, which is quite easy and requires only an 8x to 10x slide examining glass. Figures A–D are an introduction to the shapes of the maxillary palps of the families that do require that the shape be known. A few families require the recognition of ocelli; these need 20x magnification (see figure A).

Schematic of Family Hydropsychidae

Family
↓
Hydropsychidae (Common Net Spinners)
↓
Genera

Ceratopsyche & Hydropsyche (Cinnamon Caddis)	*Cheumatopsyche* (Little Olive Caddis)	*Macrostemum* (Zebra Sedge)	*Arctopsyche* (Great Gray-Spotted Sedge)
↓	↓	↓	↓
Species	Species	Species	Species
Many species all similar in size and color	Many species all similar in size and color	Few species all similar in size and color	Few species all similar in size and color

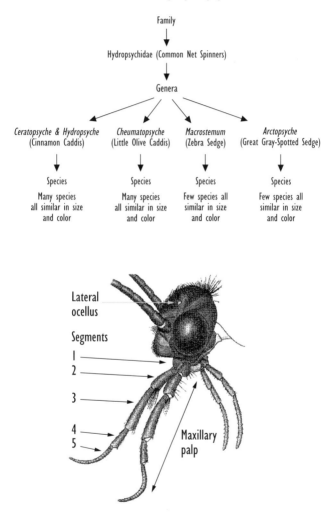

Fig. A Adult head of *Philopotamidae* (group 4 in the keys). Four families in this group.

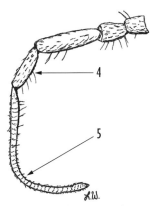

Fig. B Maxillary palp of *Hydropsychidae*, group 4, maxillary palp 5 segmented and segment 5 is at least twice as long as segment 4.

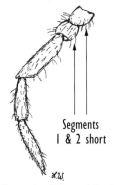

Segments
1 & 2 short

Fig. C Maxillary palp of *Rhyacophila* with segment 5 not much longer than segment 4 and segments 1 and 2 much shorter than segments 3, 4, 5.

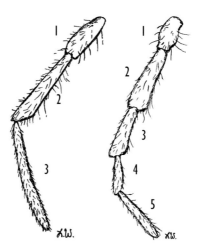

Fig. D Maxillary palps of group 6 (three families in this group including the important family *Brachycentridae*). Caddisflies with male maxillary palp 3 segmented and female maxillary palp 5 segmented.

Fisherman's Keys to the Families and Genera of Caddisflies

These keys are intended for the caddisfly families, genera, and species found in trout streams in numbers that cause good rises by trout. Many uncommon species or species found only in warm water or stillwater have been eliminated for simplicity's sake. In some cases an 8x to 10x glass will be needed for examination of the insects. These can be obtained at camera shops in the form of slide viewers. Occasionally 20x to 30x magnification will be needed for very small species; such lenses can be obtained inexpensively from BioQuip Products (see page 103). In the cases where this increased magnification is needed (keys 5 and 6), suggestions are given so that if you lack more than 8x magnification you can still identify the insect. **Note:** Size in millimeters means the overall length of the insect from the head to the tip of the wing.

Adults

A.	Caddisflies with antennae more than twice as long as bodies	go to **1**
B.	Very small caddisflies, from 2.4mm to 5.5mm	go to **2**
C.	Very large caddisflies, from 17mm to 34mm	go to **3**
D.	Caddisflies with maxillary palp 5 segmented, and segment 5 is twice as long as segment 4, figure B	go to **4**
E.	Caddisflies with segment 5 of the maxillary palp not much longer than segment 4, and	

segments 1 and 2 much shorter than
segments 3, 4, and 5, figure C   go to **5**

F. Caddisflies with male maxillary palp
3 segmented and female maxillary palp
5 segmented, figure D   go to **6**

G. Small caddisflies (5mm to 7mm)
with anterior margin of hind wing
with a row of modified hairs
in the basal half and a slight
concavity in the distal half,
figure E, bodies bright amber
with dark gray wings that
have a heavy freckling of
dark brown, E, AS, M, W.   Helicopsychidae;
Speckled Peter   *Helicopsyche borealis*

H. Medium-size caddisflies
(12mm to 15mm)
with dark gray wings
that have small scattered
light spots and dark green
to almost black bodies;
these are found only in
the East and Appalachian South.
These insects always have
maxillary palp 5 segmented
and with a single narrow
transverse wart on
the scutellum, figure F,
E, AS only.   Odontoceridae;
Dark Blue Sedge   *Psilotreta labia, P. frontalis*

I. Large caddisflies
(15mm to 17mm),
bodies are brown,

wings are gray with
a checkered pattern of
light and dark areas,
tibia of middle leg
with a pair of preapical spurs
and a row of 6 to 10 spines
on the back, figure G,
E, AS, M.
Gray Checkered Sedge

Molannidae;
Molanna uniophila,
M. tryphena

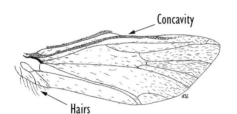

Concavity

Hairs

Fig. E

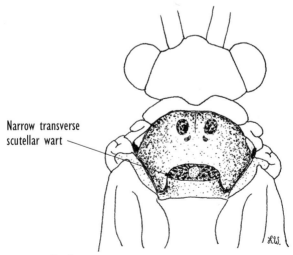

Narrow transverse
scutellar wart

Fig. F

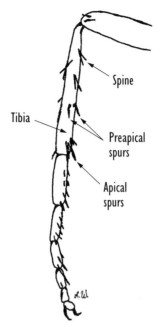

Fig. G

1. The Long-Horn Sedges and the Zebra Sedges

a.	Wings cream with faint tan markings, bodies light green, thoraxes and legs ginger, 10–17mm long, range E, AS, M. **White Millers**	Leptoceridae; *Nectopsyche albida*, *N. exquisita*, *N. diarana*
b.	Wings dark gray to dark brown, often with light patches of scales, bodies dark gray to dark brown, 11–17mm long, range E, AS, M, W. **Dark Long-Horn Sedges, aka Scaly-Winged Sedges**	Leptoceridae; *Ceraclea* spp.

c. Wings and bodies black,
9mm long; *M. alafimbriata*
can have amber bodies;
range E, AS, M, W.   Leptoceridae;
M. alafimbriata   *Mystacides sepulchralis*,
W only. **Black Dancer**   *M. alafimbriata*

---

d. Wings tan, bodies olive   Leptoceridae;
or ginger, 7–12mm long,   *Oecetis inconspicua*,
range E, AS, M, W.   *O. avara*,
Tan-Winged   *O. cinera*,
Long-Horn Sedge   *O. osteni*

---

e. Wings gray, bodies bright
blue-green (males),
golden yellow (females),
9–11mm long, range W.
Gray-Winged   Leptoceridae;
Long-Horn Sedge   *Oecetis disjuncta*

---

f. Wings black with distinctive
yellow pattern, bodies greenish
olive with black rings in
freshly emerged insects,
bodies darken with age,
15–18mm long, range   Hydropsychidae,
E, AS, M. **Zebra Sedge**   *Macrostemum zebratum*

---

2. The Microcaddisflies and Pseudo-Microcaddisflies

---

a. Tiny caddisflies, always less
than 6mm long and usually
2–4.5mm long, very hairy,
wings are narrow with long
fringes of hair (figure H),
antennae shorter than

forewings, range
E, AS, M, W.
True Microcaddisflies Hydroptilidae

Note: There are four important genera in this family: *Leucotrichia pictipes* (ring-horn microcaddis), very dark brown to black, wing with a few scattered light spots, white bands around antennae, 3–4.5mm long. *Agraylea multipunctata* (salt & pepper microcaddis), bodies green, legs dark brown, wings speckled gray and white, 3–4.5mm long. *Oxyethira pallida, O. serrata, O. michiganensis* (cream & brown microcaddis), bodies light greenish yellow, legs yellow, wings cream and brown mottled, 2–3mm long. *Hydroptila* spp. (varicolored microcaddis), bodies can be yellow, orange, and shades of brown, wings gray or brown, spotted or plain, 2.5–4mm long.

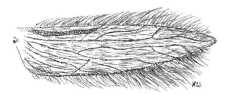

Fig. H Adult forewing *(Hydroptila hamata)*

---

b. Tiny caddisflies, 3–5mm
long, not hairy,
wings not narrow,
range E, AS, M, W. Glossosomatidae;
Pseudo-Microcaddisflies *Protoptila* spp.

Note: There are many species in this genera and colors vary considerably. The two most common colors are gray wings with cinnamon legs and bodies, and all black.

---

3. The Great Sedges and Giant Sedges

---

a. Length 19–22mm, wings cinnamon brown with dark brown to black markings, bodies and legs cinnamon brown, range E, AS, M, W. **Great Brown Autumn Sedge**

Limnephilidae;
Pycnopsyche lepida,
P. guttifer,
P. scabripennis

---

b. Length 20–22mm, wings cream and chocolate mottled, bodies dark yellow, range E, AS, M. **Chocolate & Cream Sedge**

Limnephilidae;
Platycentropus radiadus

---

c. Length 28–34mm, wings light brown and cream with a Z pattern, bodies ginger, range E, AS, M, W. **Giant Cream Pattern-Winged Sedge**

Limnephilidae;
Hydatophylax argus,
H. hesperus

---

d. Length 21–25mm, wings patterned gray, brown, and yellow, male bodies reddish brown, male maxillary palp 4 segmented, female maxillary palp 5 segmented, range E, M. **Rush Sedge**

Phryganeidae;
Phryganea cinera

---

e. Length 21–25mm, wings
reddish brown, bodies
reddish brown, male
maxillary palp 4 segmented, Phryganeidae;
range E, AS, M. W. *Ptilostomis ocellifera,*
Giant Rusty Sedge *P. semifasciata*

---

f. Length 25–28mm,
wings, legs, and bodies
ginger to brown, Limnephilidae;
range W. *Onocosmoecus frontalis,*
Great Late Summer Sedge *O. unicolor*

---

g. Length 18–34mm,
wings gray with
heavy veins, Limnephilidae;
bodies orange, *Dicosmoecus atripes,*
range W. *D. gilvipes,*
Giant Orange Sedge *D. jucundus*

---

h. Length 17–20mm,
wings dark gray with
light spotting, bodies
greenish brown to olive, Hydropsychidae;
range AS, W. *Arctopsyche grandis,*
Great Gray-Spotted Sedge *A. irrorata*

---

i. Length *H. designatus*
17–20mm, *H. incisus*
30–34mm, wings cream
and light brown with
a long silver stripe,
bodies yellow to
cinnamon, range W.
Great Silver-Striped Limnephilidae;
Sedge, aka *Hesperophylax designatus,*
Giant Golden Caddis *H. incisus*

---

4. The Net Spinners; this group includes the most important group of caddisflies for fly fishermen, Hydropsychidae (the common net spinners)

a. Maxillary palp 5 segmented and segment 5 is more than twice as long as segment 4, ocelli, scutal warts, and preapical spurs of foreleg all absent, figure I, unique wing shape.
The Super Caddisflies   Hydropsychidae

Cinnamon Caddis, aka Spotted Sedge, length 8–15mm, wings brownish gray with many tiny tan spots, bodies from almost yellow to cinnamon brown,   *Hydropsyche* and range E, AS, M, W.   *Ceratopsyche* spp.

Little Olive Caddis, aka Little Sister Sedge, length 7–12mm, wings brownish gray, usually with some tan irregular markings, bodies olive green, range E, AS, M, W.   *Cheumatopsyche* spp.

The other two important genera in the family, *Macrostemum zebratum* (zebra sedge) and *Arctopsyche grandis* and *A. irrorata* (great gray-spotted sedge) have already been covered in sections 1 and 3.

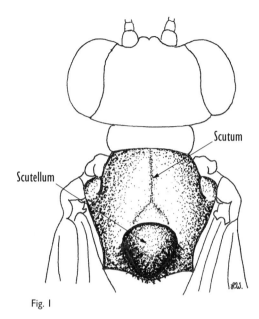

Fig. I

b. Maxillary palp 5 segmented
and segment 5 is more than
twice as long as segment 4,
figure B, ocelli absent,
scutum possesses warts
(figure J), tibia of foreleg
has a preapical spur
(figure K), 5–11mm.
**Small Yellow-Brown
Summer Sedge and
Brown-Checkered
Summer Sedge**   Polycentropodidae

Note: This family has three genera: *Neureclip-
sis crepuscularis* (little red twilight sedge),
8–9mm, bodies and legs yellow, wings reddish

brown, range E, AS, M; *Nyctiophylax celta, N. afinis, N. moestus* (dinky light summer sedge), 5–9mm, bodies and legs yellow, wings brown, range E, AS, M; *Polycentropus cinereus* (brown-checkered summer sedge), 10–11mm, bodies yellow, wings checkered light and dark brown, range E, AS, M, W.

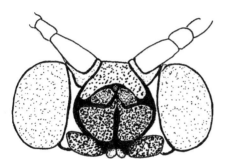

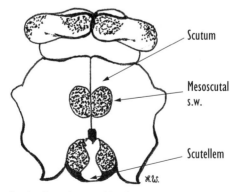

Scutum

Mesoscutal s.w.

Scutellem

Fig. J-a Dorsal view of head, pro-, and mesonotum of *Psychomyia* spp. (Psychomyiidae)

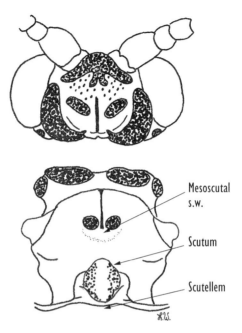

Fig. J-b Dorsal view of head, pro-, and mesonotum of *Polycentropus* spp. (Polycentropidae)

c. 5.5–10mm long, maxillary palp
5 segmented and segment 5
is more than twice as long
as segment 4 (figure B),
ocelli present (figure A),
scutum possesses warts
(figure J), tibia of foreleg
has a preapical spur (figure K).
Little Black Caddis (6–8mm),
Brown Evening Sedge (6–8mm),
Autumn Stream Sedge (9–10mm)Philopotamidae

Preapical spur

Apical spurs

Fig. K

Note: This family also has three genera important to trout fishermen. The first is *Chimarra* (tiny black caddis). This is a small black species, 5.5–8mm long. They emerge in the spring and pupae crawl to shore. Anglers in Michigan have been calling *Brachycentrus lateralis* (which emerges in midstream in huge numbers), *Chimarra*. True *Chimarra* do not usually emerge in huge numbers. The most important species of *Chimarra* are *C. aterrima*, range E, AS, M; *C. socia*, range E; *C. obscura*, range E, AS, M.

The second genus in the family is *Dolophilodes*. These are 5.5–8mm long and are also a small, dark species—very dark brown, almost black. *D. distinctus* is the E, AS, M species. It can be easily recognized by the tiny golden spots in the wings. This species emerges all year long, and in the winter and spring the females are wingless. The pupae swim to the surface and crawl onto shore, where they emerge on land. *D. aequalis* is the western species; it's important in small western streams like Rock Creek in Montana. These emerge July evenings. Early emergers are almost black but later shift to light brown.

The third genera in the family is *Wormaldia* (or *Dolophilus*). These are larger, to 10mm, and have olive brown bodies with gray or mottled brown wings. *W. anilla* is from the West and emerges in the spring and again in the fall. *W. gabriella* is also a western species and emerges from August to October. *W. moesta* is the eastern species and is a spring emerger.

---

d. 5–7mm long, maxillary palp 5 segmented and segment 5 is more than twice as long as segment 4 (figure B), ocelli absent, scutum possesses warts (figure J), tibia of foreleg lacks a preapical spur (figure K). **Tiny Dark Eastern Woodland Sedge and Tiny Yellow-Brown Sedge, aka Dinky Purple-Breasted Sedge** Psychomyiidae

Note: There are two genera in this family: *Lype diversa* is the important species, range E, AS, M; it emerges during summer evenings. They have dark brown bodies with almost black wings.

Psychomyia flavida is the second species and is 5–6mm long, range E, AS, M, W. The bodies are yellow and the wings are brown; they emerge at dark during summer evenings.

A note on this group of caddisflies with maxillary palp 5 segmented, and segment 5 twice as long as segment 4. This key involves the presence or absence of ocelli, warts, and spurs. These can be hard to see, especially on the small, dark species, without more magnification than a slide magnifier will provide. The palps can be seen with a slide magnifier. If you do not have a more powerful means of examining the insect, here is a way to be pretty sure of identifying it. The most important family in this group is Hydropsychidae. These can be easily recognized by their size, color, and unique wing shape. The Polycentropopidae are somewhat similar to Hydropsychidae but do not have the unique wing shape. The Psychomyiidae are very small; the Philopotamidae are a little larger than Psychomyiidae. If you compare the colors, sizes, range, and time of year of emergence, you should be able to differentiate the genera without a microscope.

5. The Green Sedges and the Little Black and Little Tan Short-Horn Sedges

a. Segment 5 of maxillary palp is not much longer than segment 4 and segments 1 and 2 are short, much shorter than segments 3, 4, 5

(figure C), tibia of foreleg
has apical and preapical
spurs (figure K).
Green Caddis   Rhyacophilidae

Note: This family has one genus, *Rhyacophila*.
These insects are 8–18mm long and have green
bodies and brown wings with many lighter tan
spots. There are many species found all over
the country.

---

b. Segment 5 of maxillary
palp is not much longer
than segment 4 and
segments 1 and 2 are short,
much shorter than
segments 3, 4, 5 (figure C),
tibia of foreleg lacks either
apical or preapical spurs
or both (figure K).
**Little Black and
Little Tan Short-Horn Sedge**   Glossosomatidae

Note: This family has two genera that are
important to fishermen: *Protoptila* (pseudo-
microcaddis, which we have already covered),
and *Glossosoma* (little black short-horn sedge).
They range in size 6–10mm long and the range
is E, AS, M, W. The tan species have greenish
brown bodies and tan to medium brown wings.

**6. The Chimney Case Makers, including the little
   black caddis, which is important in the spring**

---

a. Male maxillary palp
3 segmented and female
maxillary palp 5 segmented

(figure D), ocelli are absent,
scutum possesses a pair of
small separated warts
(figure L), tibia of middle leg
has an irregular row of
spines (figure G), preapical
spur or spurs on middle
tibia are one-third of
the way up from the apex
of the tibia (figure M) or without
preapical spurs, abdomen with
openings of glands on center V
in a pair of rounded, sclerotized
lobes (figure N).

**Mother's Day Caddis,
Little Black Caddis,
American Grannom,
Little Weedy Water Sedge**   Brachycentridae

Note: This family has three genera that are very
important, because they often produce swarm-
ing hatches, especially in the spring. The first
and most important is *Brachycentrus*. These
insects are 7–13mm long and have almost black
bodies with green lateral lines when freshly
emerged. They have light gray wings. The other
two genera are *Amiocentrus* and *Micrasema*,
which are 6–8mm long and similar to *Brachycentrus*, except the wings are darker.

b. Same as **a** but tibia of middle
leg lacks the row of spines and
the preapical spurs of the
middle leg are half the way
up from the apex (figure N).

Little Green-Bodied Brown-Winged Sedge, aka Little Brown Sedge

Lepitostomatidae

Note: This family has one genus, *Lepidostoma*, range E, AS, M, W. They are 9–10mm long with green bodies and dark brownish gray wings, often with a few dark spots. *L. pluviale* is the important western species and has yellow and light brown wings. Many males have a unique group of hairs with a recurve on the dorsal back half of the wings, and a hairy antennae base.

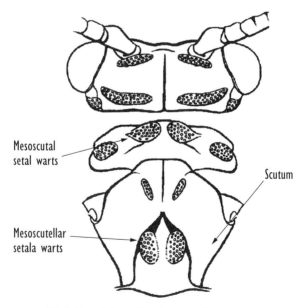

Mesoscutal setal warts

Scutum

Mesoscutellar setala warts

Fig. L Dorsal view of head, pro-, and mesonotum of *Brachycentrus* spp.

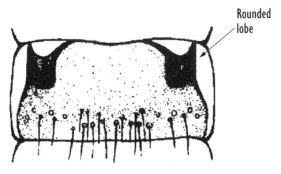

Rounded
lobe

Fig. M

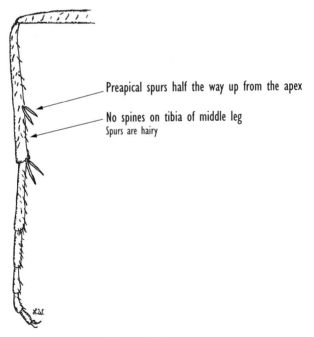

Preapical spurs half the way up from the apex

No spines on tibia of middle leg
Spurs are hairy

Fig. N Tibia of the middle leg

127

c. Male maxillary palp 3 segmented
and female maxillary palp 5 segmented
(figure D), mesioscutellum with
a single large setal wart (figure O),
tibia of foreleg has less than two spurs
(figure G), or if more then scutellum
has a single oval wart, tibia of
middle leg with one or no preapical
spurs, hind wings usually much wider
than forewings (figure P).
The Diverse Caddisflies   Limnephilidae

Note: This is a very diverse family with 14
important genera.

**A note on this group of caddisflies with
male maxillary palp 3 segmented and
female maxillary palp 5 segmented.** This
key, like the section 4 key, involves the presence or absence of structures that may be hard
to see with a slide magnifier. As on the section
4 key, you should be able to discover the family
by looking at the palps with an 8x or 10x glass
and then comparing the size, color, distribution,
and time of emergence of the insects. For
instance, if the caddisfly is 6–13mm long and
has a black body with a green lateral line and
light gray or black wings, you probably have a
Brachycentridae. If the insect is 9–10mm long
and has a green body with dark gray wings, or
in the West a yellow body with light brown
wings and the wings have the recurve, you
probably have a Lepidostomatidae. Anything
else and you probably have a Limnephilidae.

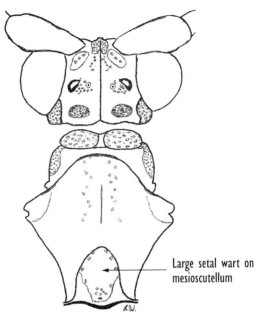

Large setal wart on mesioscutellum

Fig. O-a Dorsal view of head, pro- and mesonotum of *Limnephilus* spp. (Limnephilidae).

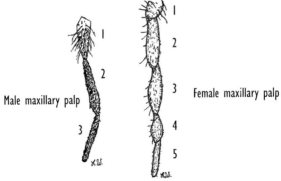

Male maxillary palp

Female maxillary palp

Fig. O-b

129

Fig. P-a Middle tibia and tarsus of *Limnephilus* spp. (Limnephilidae).

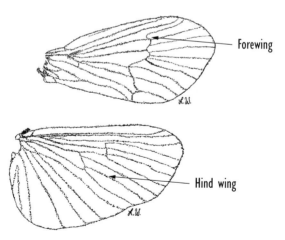

Fig. P-b Wings of *Dicosmoecus* spp. (Limnephilidae).

BIBLIOGRAPHY

Flint, O. S. Jr. 1984. The Genus Brachycentrus in North America, with a Proposed Phylogeny of the Genera of Brachycentridae (Trichoptera). Smithsonian Institution Press, *Smithsonian Contributions to Zoology* Number 398.

Hafele, Rick, and Dave Hughes. *The Complete Book of Western Hatches*. Portland, Ore.: Frank Amato Publications, 1987.

Hughes, David. *Western Streamside Guide*. Portland, Ore.: Frank Amato Publications, 1987.

Juracek, John, and Craig Mathews. *Fishing the Yellowstone Hatches*. West Yellowstone, Montana: Blue Ribbon Flies, 1992.

LaFontaine, Gary. *Caddisflies*. New York: Lyons & Burford, 1981.

Leonard, J. W., and F. A. Leonard. 1949. An Annotated List of Michigan Trichoptera. *Occasional Papers of the Museum of Zoology, University of Michigan,* 522.

———. 1949. Noteworthy Records of Caddis Flies from Michigan with Descriptions of New Species. *Papers of the Museum of Zoology, University of Michigan.*

McCafferty, W. Patrick. *Aquatic Entomology.* Boston: Jones and Bartlett, 1981.

Merritt, R. E., and K. W. Cummins, editors. *Trichoptera: An Introduction to the Aquatic Insects of North America.* Dubuque, Iowa: Kendall/Hunt Publishing Co., 1978.

Richards, Carl, and Braendle, Robert. *Caddis Super Hatches.* Portland, Ore.: Frank Amato Publications, 1997.

Ross, H. H. 1944. The Caddisflies or Trichoptera of Illinois. *State of Ill. Natural History Survey Division,* Volume 23.

Ross H. H., and J. D. Unzicker, 1965. The *Micrasema rusticum* Group of Caddisflies (Brachycentridae, Trichoptera). *Proceedings of the Biological Society of Washington* 78:251–258.

Shewey, John. *Mastering the Spring Creeks.* Portland, Ore.: Frank Amato Publications, 1994.

Solomon, Larry, and Eric Leiser. *The Caddis and the Angler.* Harrisburg, Penn.: Stackpole Books, 1977.

Wiggins, G. B. *Larvae of the North American Caddisfly Genera (Trichoptera).* Toronto and Buffalo: University of Toronto Press, 1977.

PHOTOGRAPHIC CREDITS

A book like this would have been impossible without the wonderful illustrations and photographs from all the contributors listed below.

Robert McKeon created the line drawings and silhouettes in this book, except for those in the Fisherman's Simplified Keys.

Carl Richards: 10T, 11T, 25T, 25B, 28T, 31T, 31B, 36T, 37T, 39B, 43T, 46T, 47T, 51T, 58T, 58B, 59M, 59B, 60T, 61B, 64T, 66T, 67T, 69T, 70T, 70B, 74T, 75T, 76T, 77T, 78T, 79T, 80T, 82T, 83T, 84T, 85B, 86T, 87T, 89T, 90T, 91T, 91B, 92T, 93T.

Ted Fauceglia: 12T, 12B, 68T.

Jim Schollmeyer: 26B, 27T, 28B, 32B, 34B, 38M, 38B, 53T, 53B, 54T, 54B, 55T, 55B.

Dave Hughes: cover photo, 26B, 38B, 39T, 48T, 50T.

John Juracek: 9T, 22T, 26T, 30T, 32T, 34T, 36T, 38T, 40T, 42T, 44T, 46T, 72T.

Hank Leonard: 13T.

Lindsey Wells created the line drawings in the Fisherman's Simplified Keys.

T = top   M = middle   B = bottom

PERSONAL HATCH RECORD

Caddisfly Hatches of _____

Importance	Latin Name	Common Name	Hook #	Mar	Apr	May

June	Jul	Aug	Sep	Oct	Nov	Emergence	Ovipositing

PERSONAL HATCH RECORD

Caddisfly Hatches of _____

Importance	Latin Name	Common Name	Hook #	Mar	Apr	May

June	Jul	Aug	Sep	Oct	Nov	Emergence	Ovipositing

PERSONAL HATCH RECORD

Caddisfly Hatches of _____

Importance	Latin Name	Common Name	Hook #	Mar	Apr	May

June	Jul	Aug	Sep	Oct	Nov	Emergence	Ovipositing

PERSONAL HATCH RECORD

Caddisfly Hatches of _____

Importance	Latin Name	Common Name	Hook #	Mar	Apr	May

June	Jul	Aug	Sep	Oct	Nov	Emergence	Ovipositing

PERSONAL HATCH RECORD

Caddisfly Hatches of _____

Importance	Latin Name	Common Name	Hook #	Mar	Apr	May

June	Jul	Aug	Sep	Oct	Nov	Emergence	Ovipositing

INDEX

Adult Caddis pattern, 92–93
American grannom, 125
autumn stream sedge, 120

Beadhead-Down Larva pattern, 89
black caddis, 24–25, 58–59, 94
black dancer, 19, 44–45, 55, 113
black gold-spotted caddis, 100
black long-horn sedge, 44–45
brown-checkered summer sedge, 100, 118–19
brown evening sedge, 120

caddisflies. *See also specific species*
   east of the Mississippi, 57–87
   identifying, 15–22, 102–30
   life cycle of, 9–14
   patterns, 94–99
   tying imitations, 88–91, 96–99
   west of the Mississippi, 23–56
cases, 9–10, *10*, 18
chocolate and cream sedge, 101, 115
cinnamon caddis, 15–17, 26–29, 60–63, 96–99, 117
   pattern, 95

dark blue sedge, 19, 68–69, 110
   pattern, 95
dark long-horn sedge, 19, 80–81, 112
Deep-Drifting Pupa pattern, 90
dinky light summer sedge, 101
dinky purple-breasted sedge, 100, 122
dot-winged sedge, 20, 84–85

early smoky-winged sedge, 101

giant cream pattern-winged sedge, 100, 115
giant golden caddis, 48–49, 116
giant orange sedge, 20, 50–51, 116
   pattern, 96
giant rusty sedge, 116
gray-checkered sedge, 101, 111
gray-winged long-horn sedge, 42–43, 113
great brown autumn sedge, 20, 86–87, 115
great gray-spotted sedge, 46–74, 116
great late summer sedge, 116
great silver-striped sedge, 48–49, 116
green rock worm, 38–39, 70–71
green sedge, 17–18, 38–39, 70–71, 94, 123–24

hatches, 1–2, 22
   east of the Mississippi, 57–87
   west of the Mississippi, 23–56

imitations, tying, 88–99

larvae, *9*, 15–20
little black caddis, 17, 120, 125
little black sedge, 124
little brown sedge, 20, 40–41, 126
little grannom, 18, 34–35
little gray sedge, 101
little green-bodied brown-winged sedge, 126
little olive caddis, 15–17, 30–31, 64–67, 117
little sister sedge, 30–31, 64–67, 117
little tan short-horn sedge, 124
little weedy water sedge, 125
long-horn sedges, 19

mayflies, 102
microcaddisflies, 113–14
Mother's Day caddis, 24–25, 125

October caddis, 50–51

pseudo-microcaddisflies, 113, 114–15
pupae, 10–12, *11*, 102

rush sedge, 115

scaly-winged sedge, 112
short-horn sedge, 18, 32–33, 72–73
small yellow-brown summer sedge, 118
speckled peter, 19, 36–37, 110
Spentwing Caddis pattern, 93
spotted sedge, 26–29, 117
spring creeks, 7
summer flyer, 101

tan caddis, 54, 101
tan-winged long-horn sedge, 78–79, 113
   pattern, 95
Teardrop Emerger pattern, 91
tiny black caddis, 18–19, 32–37, 100
tiny black sedge, 72–75
tiny dark eastern woodland sedge, 100, 122
tiny yellow-brown sedge, 122
traveling sedge, 53
trout lake caddis, 52–56

Underdrifting Pupa pattern, 90–91

weedy water sedge, 20, 34–35
white long-horn sedge, 82–83
white miller, 19, 82–83, 112
   pattern, 95

zebra caddis, 76–77